SSAT Upper Level Practice Tests

SSAT Upper Level Practice Tests

Three Full-Length Verbal and Quantitative
Mock Tests with Detailed Answer Explanations

ANTHEM PRESS

Anthem Press
An imprint of Wimbledon Publishing Company
www.anthempress.com

This edition first published in UK and USA 2024
by ANTHEM PRESS
75–76 Blackfriars Road, London SE1 8HA, UK
or PO Box 9779, London SW19 7ZG, UK
and
244 Madison Ave #116, New York, NY 10016, USA

© 2024

British Library Cataloguing-in-Publication Data
A catalogue record for this book is available from the British Library.

Library of Congress Control Number: 2023949173
A catalog record for this book has been requested.

ISBN-13: 978-1-83999-097-7 (Pbk)
ISBN-10: 1-83999-097-X (Pbk)

This title is also available as an e-book.

Contents

Introduction

About SSAT

The Secondary School Admission Test (SSAT) is a standardized test used by admission officers to assess the abilities of students seeking to enroll in an independent school. The SSAT measures the basic verbal, math, and reading skills students need for successful performance in independent schools. Every year, 80,000+ students take the SSAT to apply to independent schools. There are two types of SSAT administrations.

Grade Level

Students of grades 3–11 can register for one of the three SSAT tests, depending on their grades:

- The Elementary Level test is for students currently in grades 3 and 4.
- The Middle Level test is for students currently in grades 5–7.
- The Upper Level test is for students currently in grades 8–11.

The SSAT Upper has an Essay which is written by the student in response to a given writing prompt and three sections (in order of testing): Quantitative Math, Verbal Reasoning, Reading Comprehension, and each section is designed to tap into a unique aspect of a student's preparation for academic work.

How does a student arrange to take the SSAT?

Students may take the SSAT in one of the following ways:

1. **Paper SSAT:** This is the most popular and preferred option. Parents can register for paper-based test by creating an account on https://portal.ssat.org/SAP/Tests/NewRegistration.

2. **Flex Testing:** This increases the availability of the paper SSAT beyond the standard testing dates. Consider Flex testing when the standard dates or locations don't work for your schedule. There are two types of Flex testing

   - Open Flex tests—are when a school hosts a group of students for Flex testing and makes registration open to the public.

   - Closed Flex tests—are when an educational consultant or school administers the SSAT to an individual or a small group of students.

3. **At-Home Testing:** The SSAT at Home is a computer-based version of the SSAT taken on designated testing dates at pre-scheduled times.

4. **The Prometric SSAT:** This is a secure, computer-based version of the SSAT taken at Prometric test centers. It is the same reliable test as the paper and SSAT at Home versions. Note that SSAT Elementary Level is not offered by Prometric.

What types of questions are on the SSAT?

The first section, the Writing Sample, requires the student to respond to a preselected writing prompt and the next sections are composed of multiple-choice questions. The Quantitative Math and Verbal Reasoning section measure the applicant's reasoning ability.

The Verbal Reasoning test consists of two types of items: vocabulary and sentence completion.

At the Upper Level, the Quantitative Math test conforms to national mathematics standards and ask the student to identify the problem and find a solution to it. The items require one or more steps in calculating the answer.

The next section, Reading Comprehension, the student is asked to read a passage and then answer items specific to that passage.

The Essay is written by the student in response to a writing "prompt" or topic that is grade-level appropriate. The prompts rotate throughout the testing season. They are designed to prompt a student to write an informed essay on a particular topic.

The table below gives a quick snapshot of the questions in the SSAT:

Test Section	Questions	Time	Details
Writing Sample	1 Question	25 minutes	The writing sample is not scored, but schools use it to assess writing skills.
Quantitative Math	25 Questions	30 minutes	Multiple-choice questions composed of math computation based on grade-level math topics.
Reading Comprehension	40 Questions	40 minutes	Reading passages with multiple-choice questions based on the reading passages.
Verbal Reasoning	60 Questions	30 minutes	Vocabulary and analogy questions.
Quantitative Math	25 Questions	30 minutes	Multiple-choice questions composed of math computation based on grade-level math topics.

What is the format of the test? All questions are multiple choice.

What is the medium of the test? Computer based

How to use the book

- Before you start the test, read the directions for each section and note the time allocated.
- Ensure that you have a continuous block of time available to complete the entire test—including all the sections.
- When you take the practice test, remove all possible distractions including your phone.
- Take the entire test in one sitting—this is very critical for getting a realistic view of how you would do in the real test.
- Check your answers right after the test.

- Review the explanations on the same day, so you remember why you chose a particular answer.
- Before starting the next practice test, review the answers that you got wrong from the previous test and the explanations so you don't make the same mistakes.

SSAT Results

Use these attached sample reports to familiarize yourself with the SSAT score reports. You'll also find detailed explanations of each section below. There are two types of scores:

SSAT Scaled Scores: Each of the three main Elementary Level test sections is scored on a scale of 300 to 600, with a total scaled score range of 900 to 1800. Each of the three main Middle Level test sections is scored on a scale of 440 to 710, with a total scaled score range of 1320 to 2130. Each of the three main Upper Level test sections is scored on a scale of 500 to 800, with a total scaled score range of 1500 to 2400.

SSAT Percentiles: SSAT percentile rankings range between 1% and 99% and show how a student performed as compared to the other students in the same grade and of the same gender who have taken the SSAT during the past three years.

Learn more about SSAT scoring here: https://www.ssat.org/about/scoring/ssat-score-report

SSAT Upper Level Exam 1

WRITING SAMPLE

Time—25 minutes

Directions: Using two sheets of lined theme paper, plan and write an essay on the topic assigned below. DO NOT WRITE ON ANOTHER TOPIC. AN ESSAY ON ANOTHER TOPIC IS NOT ACCEPTABLE.

Topic: The influence of COVID-19 on education.

Directions: How has COVID-19 affected your education? Use reasons and specific examples to support your answer.

SECTION 2

QUANTITATIVE MATH

Time—30 minutes
25 Questions

Directions: Any figures that accompany questions in this section may be assumed to be drawn as accurately as possible EXCEPT when it is stated that a particular figure is not drawn to scale. Letters such as x, y, and n stand for real numbers.

Each question consists of a word problem followed by five answer choices. You may write in your text booklet; however, you may also be able to solve many of these problems in your head. Next, take a look at the five answer choices and select the best one.

Example	Answer
$5,413 - 4,827 =$	Ⓐ Ⓑ ● Ⓓ Ⓔ

(A) 586
(B) 596
(C) 696
(D) 1,586
(E) 1,686

The correct answer to this question is lettered A, so space A is marked.

---

1. What is 90 expressed as the product of its prime factors?

   (A) $6 \times 5 \times 3$ (B) $10 \times 3 \times 3$ (C) $9 \times 5 \times 2$ (D) $15 \times 3 \times 2$ (E) $5 \times 3 \times 3 \times 2$

2. What is the perimeter of an equilateral triangle if one side measures 14.9 cm?

   (A) 41.4 cm   (B) 43.7 cm   (C) 44.7 cm   (D) 44 cm   (E) 47.4 cm

3. How many 6 in^2 tiles can fit in a rectangular floor if the dimensions are 48 in by 12 in?

   (A) 90   (B) 96   (C) 85   (D) 100   (E) 88

4. The average weight of 8 girls in a class is 51.5 kg and the average weight of 11 boys in the same class is 56 kg. What is the average weight of all the 19 students in that class?

   (A) 51.4 kg   (B) 54.1 kg   (C) 45.1 kg   (D) 41.5 kg   (E) 54.2 kg

5. There are three equal cylindrical tanks of water in a building. If $\frac{1}{4}$ of a tank contains 650 L of water, what is the capacity of the three tanks of water together?

(A) 7,500 L   (B) 7,000 L   (C) 7,600 L   (D) 7,800 L   (E) 7,200 L

6. Five kilograms of strawberries and four kilograms of lemon cost $31.80. If one kilogram of strawberry costs $3.20, how much does one kilogram of lemon cost?

(A) $3.59   (B) $3.20   (C) $3.69   (D) $3.95   (E) cannot be determined

7. The sum of three consecutive integers is 384. What is the value of the highest number?

(A) 129   (B) 127   (C) 128   (D) 130   (E) 126

8. Mr. Rodrigo is planning to have a price markdown on the furniture he's selling. A sofa with a 35% discount now costs $364.00. What was the original price of the sofa?

(A) $650.00   (B) $506.00   (C) $565.00   (D) $560.00   (E) $655.00

9. What is the missing number in the given sequence? 1, 8, 27, 64, _____, 216, 343

(A) 125   (B) 94   (C) 89   (D) 142   (E) 180

10. Alice wants to paint a rectangular wall with an area of 64 m². How many liters of paint will she need if each liter of paint is enough to paint a dimension of 3.2 m by 2.5 m?

(A) 2 L   (B) 5 L   (C) 4 L   (D) 6.5 L   (E) 8 L

11. A water tank can hold 36 gallons. How many gallons of water does it contain when it is $\frac{2}{3}$ full?

(A) 20   (B) 24   (C) 32   (D) 30   (E) 12

12. A school wants to give each of its 25 top students a plaque of appreciation. If the plaques are in boxes of five, how many boxes do they need to purchase?

(A) 6   (B) 5   (C) 7   (D) 4   (E) 10

13. A propeller can rotate 200 times in 8 seconds. How many times can it rotate in 16 seconds?

(A) 300   (B) 350   (C) 200   (D) 250   (E) 400

14. If 120% of a number is 108, then what is the 50% of that number?

(A) 35   (B) 54   (C) 45   (D) 53   (E) 40

15. What is the value of the sum of the hundreds and ten thousandths in number 3,705.942810?

(A) 9   (B) 8   (C) 4   (D) 15   (E) 6

16. Clara and Mara finished painting their room in 120 minutes. If Clara can do the job by herself in 4 hours, how many hours will it take for Mara to finish the job alone?

    (A) 4 hours   (B) 5 hours   (C) 3.5 hours   (D) 4.5 hours   (E) 2 hours

17. What is the slope of a line that is perpendicular to the line $4x - 2y = 8$?

    (A) 2   (B) –2   (C) $\frac{1}{2}$ (D) 1   (E) $-\frac{1}{2}$

18. The width of a box is one-fourth of its length. The height of the box is one-third of its width. If the length of the box is 24 cm, what is the volume of the box?

    (A) 288 cm²   (B) 288 cm³   (C) 248 cm²   (D) 228 cm²   (E) 256 cm³

19. Marvin's test score is x more than Michael's, and Marvin's score is 78. Which of the following can be Michael's test score?

    (A) 78x (B) 78 + x (C) 78 – x (D) x – 78   (E) x + 78

20. If $\frac{2}{y}$ is subtracted from $\frac{9}{y}$, then what would be the difference?

    (A) $\frac{7}{y}$ (B) $\frac{9}{y}$ (C) $\frac{3}{y}$ (D) $\frac{5}{y}$ (E) $\frac{1}{y}$

21. What would be the value of x in the expression $\frac{8}{x} = \frac{26}{65}$?

    (A) 15   (B) 22   (C) 20   (D) 34   (E) 39

22. What is the perimeter of a square if the length of one side is 18 cm?

    (A) 72 cm   (B) 60 cm   (C) 68 cm   (D) 56 cm   (E) 76 cm

23. What is the circumference of a circle if the diameter is 14 in?

    (A) 12π in   (B) 14π in   (C) 10π in   (D) 16π in   (E) 13π in

24. The average of the four numbers is 23. What would be twice of the sum of these four numbers?

    (A) 148   (B) 154   (C) 136   (D) 184   (E) 167

25. Cleo owns an art gallery. One-fourth of the art displays are from her collection. If there are a total of 68 art displays, how many of those are from her collection?

    (A) 12   (B) 16   (C) 17   (D) 14   (E) 21

READING COMPREHENSION

Time—40 minutes
40 Questions

Directions:

This section contains seven short reading passages. Each passage is followed by several questions based on its content. Answer the questions following the passage on the basis of what is stated or implied in that passage. You may write in your test booklet.

Passage 1

New York City's Department of Education will rescind its ban on the wildly popular chatbot ChatGPT—which some worried could inspire more student cheating—from its schools' devices and networks.

In an opinion piece for Chalkbeat published Thursday, the chancellor of New York City Public Schools, David Banks, outlined the school system's plans to engage with ChatGPT, a chatbot created by artificial intelligence company OpenAI, and similar tools.

He said the ban was put in place "due to potential misuse and concerns raised by educators in our schools." However, he wrote, "the knee-jerk fear and risk overlooked the potential of generative AI to support students and teachers, as well as the reality that our students are participating in and will work in a world where understanding generative AI is crucial."

from New York City public schools remove ChatGPT ban by *Kalhan Rosenblatt, NBC News*

1. The passage is mainly about the _____.

   (A) study on how ChatGPT is useful to students

   (B) banning of ChatGPT in NY public schools

   (C) debate against the ChatGPT ban

   (D) proposal to ban ChatGPT in all public schools   (E) removal of the ChatGPT ban in NY public schools

2. Which city rescinded their ban on ChatGPT?

   (A) New York City   (B) not mentioned   (C) Upper East   (D) East Coast   (E) Brooklyn

3. Why was ChatGPT initially banned?

    (A) it's expensive

    (B) could inspire cheating or potential misuse

    (C) it needs higher level of learning

    (D) educators are not trained yet

    (E) the school system cannot adapt to the technology yet

4. Which word means similar to "rescind"?

    (A) allow (B) approve (C) life (D) enact (E) enforce

5. What is ChatGPT?

    (A) a school publication

    (B) survival kit

    (C) a cheat sheet

    (D) a chatbot created by artificial intelligence

    (E) high-tech laptop

6. What does "crucial" mean?

    (A) involving an extremely important decision or result

    (B) insignificant

    (C) not important

    (D) trivial

    (E) nonsensical

7. What is the purpose of the article?

    (A) to promote the use of ChatGPT

    (B) to disagree with the lifting of the ChatGPT ban

    (C) to persuade parents to fight against ChatGPT

    (D) to inform readers of the recent lift of the ChatGPT ban to incorporate generative AI

    (E) to cite disadvantages of allowing ChatGPT in schools

Passage 2

Caryn Marjorie wanted to talk to as many of her followers as she could—so she made an AI clone of herself.

The Snapchat influencer, who has 1.8 million subscribers, launched an AI-powered, voice-based chatbot that she hopes will "cure loneliness."

Called CarynAI, the chatbot is described on its website as a "virtual girlfriend." It allows Marjorie's fans to "enjoy private, personalized conversations" with an AI version of the influencer, the chatbot's website states.

The bot has gone viral, with Marjorie making headlines, stirring backlash and even receiving some death threats. The bot has also ignited discourse around the ethics of companion chatbots.

Marjorie, who in her Twitter bio calls herself "The first influencer transformed into AI," did not immediately respond to a request for comment.

In a tweet on Thursday, she wrote "CarynAI is the first step in the right direction to cure loneliness."

"Men are told to suppress their emotions, hide their masculinity, and to not talk about issues they are having," Marjorie, 23, wrote. "I vow to fix this with CarynAI. I have worked with the world's leading psychologists to seamlessly add [cognitive behavioral therapy] and [dialectical behavior therapy] within chats. This will help undo trauma, rebuild physical and emotional confidence, and rebuild what has been taken away by the pandemic."

from Snapchat influencer launches an AI-powered 'virtual girlfriend' to help 'cure loneliness' by *Daysia Tolentino, NBC News*

8. The passage is mainly about _____.

(A) anti-depression medications

(B) CarynAI, first AI-powered chatbot hoped will cure loneliness

(C) famous TikTok trends

(D) viral Twitter post

(E) things to do when you're bored

9. Who is Caryn Marjorie?

(A) a famous TikToker

(B) a well-known psychiatrist who uses AI to add [cognitive behavioral therapy] and [dialectical behavior therapy] within chats

(C) a Snapchat influencer who launched the first AI-powered chatbot

(D) a teacher of AI

(E) inventor of AI

10. What is the objective behind CarynAI?

    (A) make more money through interactions

    (B) gain more followers for Marjorie

    (C) study masculinity

    (D) build an AI dating community

    (E) cure loneliness through private, personalized conversations with Marjorie's AI version of herself

11. How does CarynAI achieve its objective?

    (A) with the help of social media marketing

    (B) with the help of world's leading psychologists to seamlessly add [cognitive behavioral therapy] and [dialectical behavior therapy] within chats

    (C) with the help of other social media influencers to promote the chatbot

    (D) with the help of Marjorie's professors in college

    (E) with the help of AI-generated chat responses

12. How old is Marjorie?

    (A) not mentioned   (B) in middle school   (C) 32   (D) 23   (E) 21

13. Which words means similar to "discourse"?

    (A) silence   (B) path   (C) railway   (D) discussion   (E) subject

Passage 3

When Halle Bailey was cast in the live-action remake of *The Little Mermaid*, some critics blasted the decision, proclaiming Princess Ariel could not possibly be Black.

But one professor who studies the mythology of mermaids and the present-day communities that portray them says that view couldn't be further from the truth. Yes, mermaids are mythological creatures, but their African origins are real according to Jalondra Davis, an assistant professor of English at the University of California, Riverside. And some mermaids are Black.

Part of Davis' research situates the origin of Black mermaids during the Middle Passage, a time period where Africans were enslaved and violently transported across the ocean to North America and the Caribbean. A common motif of mermaid legends is that enslaved people who went overboard transformed into water creatures along with their descendants.

In African cosmologies, "people who were lost to the water could become water spirits," Davis said. "Water spirits could take people into the water and keep them alive."

So, history informs myth. Still, according to Davis, because Black popular culture can be overly concentrated on historical dramas, it's important that there is access for Black stories that cover a range of experiences including fantasy that is not tied to fact or reality.

from Actually, Black mermaids have been part of mythology for a long time by *Uwa Ede-Osifo, NBC News*

14. Which of the following is the best sentence to insert at the end of the first sentence of the article?

    (A) how much would this movie earn?

    (B) therefore, it all makes sense that Ariel could have been Black

    (C) it is proven that Ariel could not possibly be Black

    (D) viewers were also quick to comment, and sides were chosen whether Ariel could have been Black or not

    (E) it is only a story therefore nobody is right nor wrong

15. What is the article's stand on casting Halle Bailey in the live-action remake of *The Little Mermaid*?

    (A) Ariel could possibly be Black

    (B) Ariel could not possibly be Black

    (C) there are no Black mermaids

    (D) there is no mythology talking about Black mermaids

    (E) mermaids are only Caucasian

16. What is the basis of the article's stand on Black mermaids?

    (A) stories from the locals

    (B) actual fossils and DNA samples of Black mermaids

    (C) sightings of Black mermaids in the Caribbean

    (D) African cosmologies and mythological studies

    (E) a testimony from a century-old local who claimed to have seen one

17. Which best interprets the phrase "that view couldn't be further from the truth"?

    (A) the opinion is way off the fact

    (B) the comment is definitely true

    (C) the opinion may have a possibility to be true based on facts

    (D) the opinion does not have a factual reference

    (E) it's all a hoax

18. Which best describes the overall mood of the article?

    (A) argumentative (B) sleepy (C) cheerful (D) lonely (E) informative

19. What is the purpose of the article?

(A) to disprove that Ariel could possibly be Black

(B) to share to the public studies supporting that some mermaids may be Black based on studies in mythology

(C) to discourage people from watching *The Little Mermaid*

(D) to prove that Ariel is 100% of African descent

(E) to encourage people to watch *The Little Mermaid*

Passage 4

Whey protein is marketed as having several health benefits, but research showing the full extent of each benefit (or lack thereof) is still ongoing. "Whey protein supplementation has been found to help support athletic performance in a literature review," explains Naidoo.

Whey protein is also promoted for being helpful with diabetes, immune health, asthma, and weight loss, though robust science doesn't yet back up such claims. At the very least, "whey protein is a highly bio-available source of animal protein that is absorbed quickly after ingestion," says Johnston. And protein has been shown to target muscle growth and development, strengthen bones, and help with cell growth and repair.

Despite some of whey protein's health benefits, it's classified as a dietary supplement—meaning it's only regulated by its manufacturers and isn't tested for safety or efficacy by the U.S. Food and Drug Administration (FDA) the way foods and medicines are. Indeed, Harvard Medical School warns of some "hidden dangers" in protein powders, including high amounts of sugar and calories, the presence of unknown substances, and even toxins that have been discovered in some protein powder brands.

Still, whey protein isn't known to cause harm in most adults when taken in moderate amounts, especially in the protein deficient or those needing more such as athletes, the elderly or vegetarians. Naidoo says for some such people, whey protein is an "option worth considering to supplement your protein intake," but adds that such supplementation ought to be temporary (unless directed by a physician) and shouldn't take the place of a healthy diet. "A systematic review of both experimental and randomized research studies looked at whey protein and the effect on physical health and showed that ongoing long-term use without the help of a medical or nutrition professional can cause side effects on the kidney and liver," she explains.

In other words, the best and safest way to ensure one gets enough protein is to get it from natural sources the way many do from their everyday diet. "Individuals consuming a healthy diet including all food groups are likely ingesting adequate amounts of protein," says Johnston.

from What is whey protein and is it safe to take? by *Daryl Austin, USA Today*

20. What is the main purpose of the article?

(A) to educate people of the health risks of whey protein

(B) to encourage people to buy whey protein

(C) to inform people that taking in whey protein is essential

(D) to prove that whey protein is effective in losing weight

(E) to discourage people from buying whey protein in bulk

21. Why do people take whey protein?

    (A) source of vitamin C

    (B) treat iron deficiency

    (C) weight loss and athletic performance

    (D) good for the brain

    (E) to promote sleep

22. Whey protein is best for _____.

    (A) pregnant women

    (B) protein deficient or those who need more or supplement

    (C) children below 2 years old

    (D) working individuals

    (E) those who work the night shift

23. What does long-term use of whey protein do to your body?

    (A) side effects on the kidney and liver

    (B) may cause short-term memory loss

    (C) may induce skin aging

    (D) promote hair growth

    (E) encourage cancer cell growth

24. Overall, is whey protein safe to take?

    (A) No. There are too many health risks

    (B) No. There are no proven health benefits

    (C) Yes. They are great for pregnant and lactating women

    (D) Maybe. The article does not advice whether it's safe or not

    (E) Yes. They are best taken as temporary supplement and in moderation with the help of a medical or nutrition professional

Passage 5

Goodbye humans, hello "Tessa." The US-based National Eating Disorders Association (NEDA) is making headlines after firing all its staff and replacing them with an AI-assisted chatbot called Tessa. This happened just four days after the six paid employees, who oversaw about 200 volunteers, successfully unionized. Coincidence? Oh, absolutely, Neda said; it was a long-anticipated change that had nothing to do with unionization. A blogpost written by a helpline associate begs to differ and calls the move "union busting, plain and simple."

Is this a harbinger of things to come? Are we about to see millions of jobs wiped out as humans are replaced by AI assistants with female names? After stealing all of our jobs, are the Tessas of the world going to unionize and stage a digital takeover of Earth?

The short answer is: maybe. All emerging technology goes through the "Gartner hype cycle"; now, we're at the inflated expectations and breathless predictions stage of that cycle and heading towards the "trough of disillusionment" before things supposedly level out. I don't think AI will lead to the end of civilization as we know it in the near future. But I do think an awful lot of corporations are champing at the bit to replace as many expensive humans as they can with AI and will use the new technology as a way to clamp down on a recent wave of labor organizing. In the next few years, I think we are going to see a lot of chaotic experimentation as companies rush to cost-cut and bring their own "Tessas" to market.

from Will AI free us from drudgery—or leave us jobless and hungry? by *Arwa Mahdawi, The Guardian*

25. What is the article about?

   (A) the advantages of AI in the economy

   (B) the effectiveness of Tessa

   (C) the future of NEDA after firing all of its paid employees

   (D) the backstory of AI

   (E) the author's opinion on the future of labor and AI

26. What is "Tessa"?

   (A) AI-assisted chatbot

   (B) the CEO of NEDA

   (C) the author of the passage

   (D) the name of the AI responsible for many chatbots

   (E) the company's name who started the AI

27. Which best describes the mood of the writer regarding the topic?

   (A) cheerful   (B) lonely   (C) opinionated   (D) sorrowful   (E) joyous

28. Which sentence best concludes the article?

   (A) AI may not end civilizations, but more jobs will be replaced in the near future as AI continues to improve

   (B) AI can never fully function without a human employee

   (C) AI is unable to 100% take a paid employee's job

   (D) There's still a long way to go with AI

   (E) It will be impractical for companies to replace paid employees with AI

29. What does "harbinger" mean?

(A) conceitedly assertive and dogmatic in one's opinions

(B) anything that foreshadows a future event

(C) the method used or steps taken

(D) nearness in space, position, degree, or relation

(E) something that happens as a consequence

Passage 6

Well, it was a cloudy day at that time of year when days begin to be rather short and rather cold- when it is almost too dark at team time to set the table till the nursery lamp is lighted, and when mamma and Nurse begin to take last year's warm frocks and coats from the upper shelves in the nursery wardrobe, where they had been put in the spring, and to call the children away from their play very often in the course of a morning, and beg them to stand still a few minutes while last year's frocks are tried on- but always on the wrong children. This, you all know, is a little tiresome, and puzzling too, for it makes you half think you are turning into your elder sister, and that it is the next younger one who is going to be you.

Interruptions of this kind had been going on all the morning in Cissa's nursery, and she had not minded it very much, though Nurse had kept her standing quite half an hour, while she fitted Violet's purple frock on her little person, and stuck-Cissa thought- hundreds of pins into the stuff, and one now and then into Cissa's soft white neck and pinky arms as well.

from Cissa's Black Cat by *A. Keary*

30. Who is the main character of the story?

(A) nurse (B) mamma (C) Cissa (D) Violet (E) nursery

31. Which season is implied by the phrase "at that time of year when days begin to be rather short and rather cold"?

(A) summer (B) spring (C) winter (D) rainy (E) hot

32. Which best describes what the phrase "you are turning into your elder sister, and that it is the next younger one who is going to be you" mean?

(A) getting another sibling

(B) transforming into another person

(C) getting older

(D) getting younger

(E) staying the same age

33. What does "frock" mean?

    (A) a pair of trousers

    (B) a gown or dress

    (C) a headpiece

    (D) a glove worn in the hands

    (E) a hat

34. Which word is mostly similar to "puzzling"?

    (A) confusing   (B) smart   (C) dexterous   (D) straightforward   (E) basic

Passage 7

A secluded and mountainous part of Stiria there was, in old time, a valley of the most surprising and lux-uriant fertility. It was surrounded, on all sides, by steep and rocky mountains, rising into peaks, which were always covered with snow, and from which a number of torrents descended in constant cataracts. One of these fell westward, over the face of a crag so high, that, when the sun had set to everything else, and all below was darkness, his beams still shone full upon this waterfall, so that it looked like a shower of gold. It was therefore, called by the people of the neighborhood, the Golden River. It was strange that none of these streams fell into the valley itself. They call descended on the other side of the mountains and wound away through broad plains and by populous cities. But the clouds were drawn so constantly to the snowy hills, and rested so softly in the circular hollow, that in time of drought and heat, when all country round was burnt up, there was still rain in the little valley; and its crops were so heavy, and its hay so high, and its apples so red, and its grapes so blue, and its wine so rich, and its honey so sweet, that is was a marvel to everyone who beheld it, and was commonly called the Treasure Valley.

from The King of the Golden River *by John Ruskin, LL.D.*

35. What is the story about?

    (A) about the neighborhood that benefitted from the valley

    (B) about the owner of the valley

    (C) about the animals that inhabited the valley

    (D) about a valley with beautiful scenery and fertile land

    (E) about the gold mine in the valley

36. Which implies why the valley was called the Treasure Valley?

    (A) there is gold in the valley

    (B) there is a diamond mine in the valley

    (C) the trees bear money

    (D) the leaves of plants that grow in the valley turn into gold

    (E) even when the country was burnt up, the valley still grows luscious produce and sweet honey

37. Which best describes the scenery from the story?

    (A) full and vibrant (B) gray and gloomy (C) wet and sad (D) red and arid (E) dry and hot

38. Which best explains the phrase "a valley of the most surprising and luxuriant fertility"?

    (A) there are many children born in the valley

    (B) women who come to the valley get pregnant

    (C) livestock produce many offspring

    (D) the land is fertile, and crops thrive well

    (E) animals come here to reproduce

39. Which implies why the stream was called the Golden River?

    (A) there are specks of gold in the riverbed

    (B) as the sun sets, beams still shone full upon the waterfall

    (C) the water turns gold when collected

    (D) the river points to a pot of gold

    (E) the riverbed is made of gold

39. What does "populous" mean?

    (A) only a few people (B) heavily populated (C) ostentatiously lofty (D) luxurious (E) delectable

SECTION 4

VERBAL REASONING

Time—30 minutes
60 Questions

Directions: This section is divided into two parts that contain different types of questions. As soon as you have completed part one, answer the questions in part two. You may write in your test booklet. For each answer you select, fill in the corresponding circle on your answer document.

PART ONE

Directions: Each question in part one is made up of a word in capital letters followed by five choices. Choose a word that is most nearly the same in meaning as the word in capital letter.

Example   Answer
SWIFT: (A) clean   (B) fancy   (C) fast   (D) quiet   (E) noisy   Ⓐ Ⓑ ● Ⓓ Ⓔ

---

1. AMIABLE

   (A) friendly   (B) bad   (C) cold   (D) mean   (E) hostile

2. ALOOF

   (A) having tender feelings   (B) emotionally distant   (C) charitable

   (D) big-hearted   (E) satisfactory

3. APATHETIC

   (A) having great affection or love

   (B) characterized by or expressing goodwill

   (C) showing no interest or concern

   (D) having tender feelings

   (E) acting in a manner that causes the least harm

4. ABDUCT

   (A) give   (B) give up   (C) let go   (D) snatch   (E) release

5. ABSURD

(A) logical (B) foolish (C) practical (D) realistic (E) sensible

6. ACCLAIM

(A) to hold responsible

(B) to criticize or reproach in a harsh or vehement manner

(C) to announce or proclaim with enthusiastic approval

(D) to judge or discuss the merits and faults of

(E) to form an opinion or estimate

7. ADAGE

(A) proverb (B) adjunct (C) appendix (D) auxiliary (E) annex

8. ADJOURN

(A) advance (B) carry out (C) expedite (D) discontinue (E) convene

9. ADMONISH

(A) allow (B) compliment (C) flatter (D) reprimand (E) laud

10. ADVERSARY

(A) someone who offers opposition

(B) a person who associates or cooperates with another

(C) a person who is subordinate to another in rank

(D) something that aids and supplements another

(E) a person who bets on a competitor in a race

11. BOISTEROUS

(A) calm (B) moderate (C) quiet (D) soft (E) unruly

12. BREVITY

(A) shortness of time or duration

(B) a long individual life

(C) tenure

(D) the ability to last over time

(E) the ability or strength to continue

13. BLISS

   (A) dullness or inactivity

   (B) distress or suffering caused by need

   (C) utter joy or contentment

   (D) wretchedness of condition

   (E) a cause or occasion of grief or regret

14. BLUNT

   (A) pointed   (B) polite   (C) sharp   (D) dull   (E) subtle

15. BLEAK

   (A) bright   (B) grim   (C) cheerful   (D) friendly   (E) sympathetic

16. BLUNDER

   (A) make flawless or faultless

   (B) to move or act blindly

   (C) make better

   (D) to make fully skilled

   (E) to make provision or look out

17. BOORISH

   (A) delicate   (B) gentle   (C) rude   (D) kind   (E) mannerly

18. BANTER

   (A) flatter   (B) praise   (C) charm   (D) tease   (E) compliment

19. BRISK

   (A) idle   (B) inactive   (C) lazy   (D) lethargic   (E) lively

20. BRINK

   (A) center   (B) middle   (C) interior   (D) inside   (E) edge

21. CACHE

   (A) money   (B) hoard   (C) public   (D) uncover   (E) squander

22. COAX

    (A) to attempt to influence by gentle persuasion, flattery

    (B) to deprive of courage, hope, or confidence

    (C) to drive or force back

    (D) to repel with denial

    (E) persuade not to do something

23. CAPRICIOUS

    (A) cautious   (B) constant   (C) predictable   (D) erratic   (E) reliable

24. CASCADE

    (A) to spring clear of the ground

    (B) to rise suddenly or quickly

    (C) to leap

    (D) to fall in a rush

    (E) to spring over

25. COLLIDE

    (A) fail   (B) lose   (C) crash   (D) lose   (E) mend

26. COMPEL

    (A) block   (B) dissuade   (C) discourage   (D) halt   (E) urge

27. CONDONE

    (A) to apply oneself

    (B) to disregard or overlook

    (C) to refuse to agree

    (D) to withhold something from

    (E) to refuse to recognize

28. CONTEMPLATE

    (A) ponder   (B) forget   (C) ignore   (D) neglect   (E) reject

29. CONTEND

    (A) oppose   (B) agree   (C) comply   (D) retreat   (E) surrender

30. CONVENE

    (A) disperse (B) divide (C) gather (D) scatter (E) separate

PART TWO

Directions: Each question below is made up of a sentence with one or two blanks. One blank indicates that one word is missing. Two blanks indicate that two words are missing. Each sentence is followed by four choices. Select a word or pair of words that will best complete the meaning of the sentence as a whole.

Example   Answer

Ann carried the box carefully so that she would not _____ the pretty glasses.   ●ⒷⒸⒹ

(A) break
(B) fix
(C) open
(D) stop

Example   Answer

When our boat first crashed into the rocks we were _____, but we soon felt   ●ⒷⒸⒹ
_____ when we realized that nobody was hurt.

(A) afraid; relieved
(B) happy; confused
(C) sleepy; sad
(D) sorry; angry

---

31. He would have preferred to _____ away the afternoon than sit in this boring class.

    (A) litter (B) liter (C) loiter (D) lottery

32. A dog was found under the _____ after the strong earthquake.

    (A) debris (B) debt (C) debit (D) dearth

33. After almost a _____, she still comes to the port hoping the day will come when he will come home.

    (A) minute (B) decade (C) destiny (D) dream

34. There is no greater betrayal for Tim than his best friend _____ him into investing in his pyramid scam.

    (A) approving (B) deluding (C) debating (D) denying

35. She did not consider her disability a _____ for her to live a better life.

    (A) advantage (B) edge (C) opportunity (D) deficit

36. You can get _____ from the extreme summer heat so carry water everywhere.

    (A) rich (B) wet (C) dehydration (D) advantage

37. He deserved to rot in jail for being a _____ man.

    (A) despicable (B) honest (C) benevolent (D) generous

38. These beautiful species continue to _____ in number as humans continue to pollute the world.

    (A) diminish (B) increase (C) spike (D) develop

39. The court proved her guilty that she acted on her own will _____ her agency's involvement from her inappropriate behavior.

    (A) agreeing (B) disclaiming (C) confirming (D) concurring

40. Involve yourself into intelligent _____ rather than meaningless gossips.

    (A) decision (B) journey (C) discourse (D) dissuade

41. It was an _____ day for our team because the game was scheduled on a _____ weather.

    (A) lucky; dismal (B) unlucky; great (C) fortunate; terrible (D) unfortunate; dismal

42. The opposition _____ a _____ on the outcome of today's hearing.

    (A) submitted; dispute (B) submitting; disputes (C) submit; disputes (D) submitted; disputes

43. The government _____ the media to _____ information on the current debate against the neighboring nation.

    (A) allowed; draft (B) opened; discourage (C) forbade; disseminate (D) entered; foresee

44. With the current _____ in the economy, many people _____ to unconventional occupations to earn more.

    (A) decrease; leave (B) fluctuate; repel (C) shift; divert (D) stability; stay

45. The stadium was _____ with _____ cheering when the home team won the game.

    (A) emptied; silent (B) filled; ecstatic (C) absent; shrilling (D) full; humble

46. She was eyeing for an _____ goal that was too hard to _____.

 (A) elusive; achieve   (B) easy; reach   (C) difficult; fail   (D) challenging; lose

47. Her eyes _____ at the beautifully _____ crown.

 (A) closed; decorated   (B) opened; ruined   (C) twitched; burnt   (D) sparkled; embellished

48. It will be his _____ acting break to _____ the main protagonist of the play.

 (A) biggest; enact   (B) smallest; host   (C) littlest; write   (D) largest; show

49. The research _____ the _____ of gadget use and electronics exposure to toddlers.

 (A) studies; affect   (B) encompass; affect   (C) encompasses; effects   (D) study; effect

50. The children's disappearance is an _____ that has caused great _____ to the community.

 (A) achievement; success   (B) enigma; distress   (C) puzzle; joy   (D) accomplishment; reward

51. Coffee is to beverage as salt is to _____.

 (A) salty   (B) seasoning   (C) white   (D) crystal

52. Car is to fuel as cellphone is to _____.

 (A) technology   (B) communication   (C) battery   (D) charger

53. Soap is to body as shampoo is to _____.

 (A) hair   (B) bottle   (C) bathroom   (D) liquid

54. Accept is to reject as send is to _____.

 (A) message   (B) phone   (C) receive   (D) email

55. Towel is to dry as kettle is to _____.

 (A) stainless steam   (B) steam   (C) boil   (D) electric

56. Train is to vehicle as table is to _____.

 (A) wood   (B) dining   (C) round   (D) furniture

57. Fire is to heat as ice is to _____.

 (A) cold   (B) refrigerator   (C) North Pole   (D) cube

58. Fish is to swim as horse is to _____.

    (A) gallop (B) mammal (C) mane (D) farm

59. Tiny is to small as giant is to _____.

    (A) fantasy (B) large (C) cute (D) scary

60. Cut is to shorten as extend is to _____.

    (A) brief (B) deadline (C) prolong (D) railway

QUANTITATIVE MATH

Time—30 minutes

25 Questions

Directions: Each question is followed by five suggested answers. Read each question and then decide which one of the five suggested answers is best.

Find the row of spaces on your answer document that has the same number as the question. In this row, mark the space having the same letter as the answer you have chosen. You may write in your test booklet.

Example

5,413 – 4,827 =

(A) 586
(B) 596
(C) 696
(D) 1,586
(E) 1,686

Answer

● (B) (C) (D) (E)

The correct answer to this question is lettered A, so space A is marked.

---

1. How many factors does 36 have?

   (A) 9   (B) 5   (C) 12   (D) 7   (E) 3

2. The angles of a pentagon form an arithmetic sequence. The smallest angle measures 70°. What does the largest angle measure?

   (A) 158°   (B) 125°   (C) 70°   (D) 140°   (E) 146°

3. If you add the reciprocals of 0.2 and 0.9, what would be the sum?

   (A) $\frac{110}{9}$ (B) $2\frac{1}{9}$ (C) $6\frac{1}{9}$ (D) $\frac{54}{9}$ (E) $6\frac{1}{18}$

4. The area of the rectangle ABCD below is 240 cm². If E is the midpoint of AB, what is the area of the shaded part?

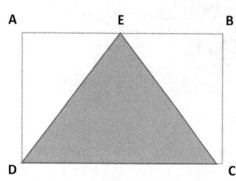

(A) 120 cm² (B) 60 cm² (C) 180 cm² (D) 90 cm² (E) cannot be determined

5. If $27x + 3y = 124$ and $x - z = 18$, then what is the value of x?

(A) 9 (B) 5 (C) 11 (D) 3 (E) cannot be determined

6. Three consecutive odd integers have sum 477. What is the sum of the smallest and largest of the three integers?

(A) 316 (B) 318 (C) 320 (D) 322 (E) 315

7. When 67,234 is divided by 392, the result is closest to?

(A) 168 (B) 175 (C) 160 (D) 172 (E) 167.5

8. Subtract $(3x + 2y - 6z)$ from $(8x - 5y + 2z)$

(A) $11x - 3y - 4z$ (B) $11x + 3y + 4z$ (C) $5x - 7y + 8z$ (D) $5x - 7y - 8z$ (E) $5x - 3y + 4z$

9. If $2\dfrac{11}{19}$ is written as an improper fraction, what will be the numerator be?

(A) 19 (B) 11 (C) 49 (D) 22 (E) 34

10. A cow eats 1.5 kg of oats and 2.5 kg of grass each day. If the cow has eaten a total of 20 kg, how many kg of grass has been eaten?

(A) 12.5 kg (B) 7.5 kg (C) 12 kg (D) 8 kg (E) 10 kg

11. Lisa has bought a dress for $52.64, a pair of shoes for $37.03, and a bag for $84.75. How much did she spend in total?

(A) $174.24 (B) $147.42 (C) $147.24 (D) $174.04 (E) $174.42

12. The cube below has a side length of 6 in. Give the surface area.

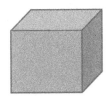

(A) 216 in² (B) 261 in² (C) 36 in² (D) 260 in² (E) 206 in²

13. A right triangle has a hypotenuse of 13 m, and one leg is 12 m. What is the length of the other leg?

(A) 1 m (B) 10 m (C) 5 m (D) 8 m (E) 4 m

14. Give the y-intercept, if there is one of the graph of the equation $y = 5(x - 1)^2 + 2(x - 3)$.

(A) (0, 1) (B) (0, –2) (C) (0, 2) (D) (0, –1) (E) (0, 0)

For questions 15 and 16, please refer to the graph below.

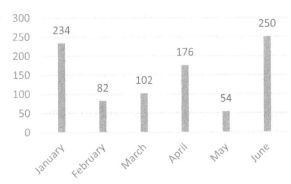

Number of Books Borrowed in Sinclair's Library (Year 2022)

15. How many more books were borrowed in the month of June than in March?

(A) 102 books (B) 148 books (C) 176 books (D) 140 books (E) 82 books

16. Suzanne, the Librarian of Sinclair Library, was doing a bi-annual inventory and wants to know how many books were borrowed. How many books were borrowed from January until June of 2023?

(A) 898 (B) 889 (C) 988 (D) 998 (E) cannot be determined

17. The Rai Library is ordering some bookshelves. If x is the number of bookshelves they want to order, which each cost $170.00 and there is a one-time delivery charge of $350.00, which of the following represents the total cost, in dollar, per bookshelf?

(A) $170 + 350x$ (B) $170x + 350$ (C) $\dfrac{170x + 350}{x}$ (D) $\dfrac{170x + 350}{170}$ (E) $170x - 350$

18. A regular pentagon has perimeter of 24 m. Give the length of one side in mm.

(A) 4800 mm   (B) 4800 cm   (C) 4000 cm   (D) 4.8 mm   (E) 4200 mm

19. One side of a square is equal to $x + 8$. Give its perimeter in terms of x.

(A) $4x + 8$ (B) $x + 32$ (C) $4x - 32$ (D) $4x + 32$ (E) $4x + 16$

20. A circle on a coordinate plane has an equation of $x^2 + y^2 = 324$. Which of the following is the circle's circumference?

(A) 30π (B) 36π (C) 18π (D) 15π (E) 24π

21. A circle on a coordinate plane has an equation of $x^2 + y^2 = 576$. Which of the following is the circle's circumference?

(A) 24π (B) 58π (C) 48π (D) 33π (E) 48

22. A circle on a coordinate plane has an equation of $x^2 + y^2 = 45$. What would be the area of the circle?

(A) 79π (B) 90π (C) 63π (D) 45π (E) 54π

23. In a jar, there are 5 blue marbles, 7 red marbles, 11 green marbles. If Ysabel reaches her hand in the jar and grabs one marble, what is the likelihood she will pick up a blue marble?

(A) $\dfrac{5}{23}$ (B) $\dfrac{7}{23}$ (C) $\dfrac{11}{23}$ (D) $\dfrac{17}{23}$ (E) $\dfrac{2}{23}$

24. The volume of a sphere is 250 cubic in. What is the diameter of the sphere? (Round off to nearest tenths if applicable)

(A) 8.92 in   (B) 7.82 in   (C) 7.28 in   (D) 8.29 in   (E) 7.47 in

25. In a math contest, there are five students who competed—Troy, Nathan, Cass, Lilian, and Quincy. Troy outscored Nathan by 17 points; Nathan outscored Quincy by 21 points; Lilian outscored Nathan by 49 points and Cass by 23 points. Who came in third among the five?

(A) Quincy   (B) Lilian   (C) Nathan   (D) Cass   (E) Troy

Answer Key

Section 1

Topic: The influence of COVID-19 on education.

Who would have thought that a time will come when many things we do outside will be done inside the comforts of our homes. From working a full-time job, seeing a doctor, and even completing a school year or better yet graduating, can now be done at home.

All of these may have been brought by the pandemic, which is something nobody wished to happen, but it only proves how we as a civilization can adapt to almost anything thrown at us. It also proves how technology has improved and definitely made lives more convenient.

Don't get me wrong. The rise of technology did a terrible thing to the world, but you have to admit, one cannot imagine living without technology. Without technology, you would have been sitting the same school year for 2–3 years waiting for the pandemic to clear out. It made it possible to continue learning and moving forward despite being confined at home. Because we were not spending more time preparing for the day or traveling to school, there was more time for studies, recreation at home, and expanding your knowledge. It was possible to learn at your own pace and many had extra time in their hands to learn a new skill or start a new hobby.

However, it was also a time of loneliness and for some, passive learning. There is too little opportunity to stay in touch with friends therefore it made it challenging to maintain or build a relationship. After all, social well-being is part of your holistic health. Some may have found a way to cope but many didn't. Not all institutions were created equal therefore, not everybody was prepared for the switch which made them ineffective in remote learning. There are students who cannot afford remote learning therefore, some of them had to go through a different approach. Some of them had to go through a difficult decision of skipping the school year. Some will say those were the worst among their school years.

As for me, it is a great opportunity to have the option to continue remote learning now that the pandemic is over. However, I believe that it should still continue to be an option and not the only way. We should make options for both remote and face-to-face learning so that students may choose which may work best for them. In the end, the goal is to access education the best way possible for you.

How did it affect you? What did you do to cope?

Section 2

1. E	6. D	11. B	16. A	21. C
2. C	7. A	12. B	17. E	22. A
3. B	8. D	13. E	18. B	23. B
4. B	9. A	14. C	19. C	24. D
5. C	10. E	15. D	20. A	25. D

1.   Answer: E

The prime factors of a number are the set of prime numbers which when multiplied together give the actual number. Among the choices, only option E consists of prime numbers and when multiplied will result in 90, hence the answer is E.

2.   Answer: C

To get the perimeter of an equilateral triangle, use the formula $P = 3s = 3(14.9) = 44.7$. The perimeter of the equilateral triangle is 44.7 cm, hence the answer is C.

3.   Answer: B

Let's get the area of the rectangle first. $A = l \times w = 48 \times 12 = 576$ in². Now that we got the area of the rectangle, divide it to 6 in² next: 576 in² ÷ 6 in² = 96. It can fit 96 6 in² tiles, hence the answer is B.

4.   Answer: B

Let's get first the sum of the weight of all students. The sum of the weight for girls: $8 \times 51.5 = 412$. The sum of the weight for boys: $11 \times 56 = 616$. The sum for all students: $412 + 616 = 1,028$. Next, divide it with the total number of students; $\dfrac{1028}{19} = 54.1$. The average weight for all students is 54.1 kg, hence the answer is B.

5.   Answer: C

Let's get the capacity of one tank: $650 \times 4 = 2,600$. Since one tank can contain 2,600 L, multiply it by 3 to get the total capacity: $2,600 \times 3 = 7,800$. The three tanks can hold 7,800 L, hence the answer is C.

6.   Answer: D

Multiply the cost of the strawberries to the number of kilograms: $3.20 × 5 = $16.00. Subtract the result from the total cost: $31.80 – $16.00 = $15.80. Divide the difference with the number of kilograms of lemon: $15.80 ÷ 4 = $3.95. One kilogram of lemon costs $3.95, hence the answer is D.

7.   Answer: A

Let x be the first integer, $x + 1$ be the second integer, and $x + 2$ be the third integer: Add the three integers: $x + x + 1 + x + 2 = 384 \Rightarrow 3x + 3 = 384 \Rightarrow 3x = 381 \Rightarrow x = 127$. Now that we have the value of x, let's substitute to get the highest number: $x + 2 = 127 + 2 = 129$. The highest number is 129, hence the answer is A.

8.   Answer: D

Let x be the original price. Use the formula $original\ price = \dfrac{discounted\ price}{1 - discount\ rate} \Rightarrow x = \dfrac{364}{1 - 0.35} \Rightarrow x = \dfrac{364}{0.65} \Rightarrow x = 560$. The original price is $560.00, hence the answer is D.

9.   Answer: A

The sequence follows the cubed of a number: $1^3 = 1$, $2^3 = 8$, $3^3 = 27$, $4^3 = 64$. The next number will be 5 and its cubed is 125, hence the answer is A.

10. Answer: E

   Let's get the area that each liter of paint can cover: 3.2 × 2.5 = 8 m². Divide it with the area of the wall: 64 m² ÷ 8 m² = 8. Alice will need 8 liters of paint, hence the answer is E.

11. Answer: B

   Multiply the total capacity of water to the fraction: $36 \times \dfrac{2}{3} = 24$. There will be 24 gallons in the water tank, hence the answer is B.

12. Answer: B

   Since one box can fit five plaques, divide it with the total number of students: 25 ÷ 5 = 5. They need to purchase 5 boxes, hence the answer is B.

13. Answer: E

   Simply multiply 200 by 2, since 16 is twice 8: 200 × 2 = 400. The propeller can rotate 400 times in 16 seconds, hence the answer is E.

14. Answer: C

   Let x be the number. $1.2x = 108 \implies x = 90$. The number is 90 and half of it or 50% is 45, hence the answer is C.

15. Answer: D

   The hundreds place is 7 and the ten thousandths place is 8. Let's add: 7 + 8 = 15. The sum is 15, hence the answer is D.

16. Answer: A

   Let x the number of minutes that will take Mara to paint their room: $\dfrac{1}{x} + \dfrac{1}{240} = \dfrac{1}{120} \implies \dfrac{1}{x} = \dfrac{1}{120} - \dfrac{1}{240}$ $\implies \dfrac{1}{x} = \dfrac{1}{240}$. Mara can finish the job alone in 240 minutes or 4 hours, hence the answer is A.

17. Answer: E

   The slope of a line perpendicular to a given line is the negative reciprocal of the slope of the given line. Let's get the slope of the given line: $y = mx + b \implies -2y = -4x + 8 \implies y = 2x - 4$. The slope is 2. The negative reciprocal of 2 is $-\dfrac{1}{2}$, hence the answer is E.

18. Answer: B

   Let's get the dimensions of the box. The length is 24 cm, the width (which is $\dfrac{1}{4}$ of the length) is 6 cm and the height (which is $\dfrac{1}{3}$ of the width) is 2 cm. To get the volume, use the formula: $V = l \times w \times h =$ 24 × 6 × 2 = 288 cm³. The volume of the box is 288 cm³, hence the answer is B.

19. **Answer: C**

    Michael's score is less than Marvin's score. If Marvin's score is 78, then Michael's score can only be $78 - x$, hence the answer is C.

20. **Answer: A**

    The given fractions have similar denominator. Subtract: $\dfrac{9}{y} - \dfrac{2}{y} = \dfrac{7}{y}$. The difference is $\dfrac{7}{y}$, hence the answer is A.

21. **Answer: C**

    Apply cross-multiplication to get the value of x: $26x = 520 \Rightarrow x = 20$. The value of x is 20, hence the answer is C.

22. **Answer: A**

    To get the perimeter of a square, use the formula $P = 4s = 4(18) = 72$ cm. The perimeter is 72 cm, hence the answer is A.

23. **Answer: B**

    To get the circumference of a circle, use the formula $C = 2\pi r$ or $C = d\pi$. Since the diameter was given, we will use $C = d\pi = 14\pi$. The circumference of the circle is 14π in, hence the answer is B.

24. **Answer: D**

    Let's get the sum of the four number: $23 \times 4 = 92$. Now that we have the sum, multiply it by two: $92 \times 2 = 184$. The answer is D.

25. **Answer: D**

    Let x be the number of art displays that are from Cleo's collection: $56 \left(\dfrac{1}{4}\right) = x \Rightarrow x = 14$. 14 of the art displays are from Cleo's collection, hence the answer is D.

Section 3

1. E	6. A	11. B	16. D	21. C	26. A	31. C	36. E
2. A	7. D	12. D	17. C	22. B	27. C	32. C	37. A
3. B	8. B	13. C	18. E	23. A	28. D	33. B	38. D
4. C	9. C	14. D	19. B	24. E	29. B	34. A	39. B
5. D	10. E	15. A	20. A	25. E	30. B	35. D	40. B

1.   The correct answer is E. The passage is about the decision to remove the recent ban placed on the use of ChatGPT in New York City Public Schools.

2.   The correct answer is A. New York City's Department of Education will rescind its ban on the widely popular chatbot ChatGPT.

3.   The correct answer is B. David Banks outlined the school system's plans to engage with ChatGPT, a chatbot created by artificial intelligence company OpenAI, and similar tools.

4.   The correct answer is C. To rescind means to declare null and void. Synonyms are to lift, abolish, and cancel.

5.   The correct answer is D. David Banks outlined the school system's plans to engage with ChatGPT, a chatbot created by artificial intelligence company OpenAI, and similar tools.

6.   The correct answer is A. The ban was put in place "due to potential misuse and concerns raised by educators in our schools."

7.   The correct answer is D. The passage is about the decision to remove the recent ban placed on the use of ChatGPT in New York City Public Schools to support students and teachers, as well as the reality that understanding AI is crucial.

8.   The correct answer is B. The passage is about the viral AI-powered, voice-based chatbot launched by Caryn Marjorie, a Snapchat influencer, which she hopes will "cure loneliness" through private, personalized conversations with an AI version of herself.

9.   The correct answer is C. Caryn Marjorie, a Snapchat influencer, is the inspiration of CarynAI. She launched the AI-powered, voice-based chatbot hoping will "cure loneliness" especially in men.

10. The correct answer is E. CarynAI allows Marjorie's fans to "enjoy private, personalized conversations" which she hopes will cure loneliness. She promotes men to talk about issues and not suppress their emotions.

11. The correct answer is B. Marjorie said that she has worked with the world's leading psychologists to seamlessly add [cognitive behavioral therapy] and [dialectical behavior therapy] within chats. This will help undo trauma, rebuild physical and emotional confidence, and rebuild what has been taken away by the pandemic.

12. The correct answer is D. "Men are told to suppress their emotions, hide their masculinity, and to not talk about issues they are having," Marjorie, 23, wrote.

13. The correct answer is C. Discourse means communication of thought by words; talk; conversation.

14. The correct answer is D. The next sentence introduces one professor who claimed that there would have been Black mermaids based on African slavery history which inspired the research on mermaid's Black origins. Sentence D would be the best sentence to follow the critics' comments that Ariel could not possibly be Black to show that there are two sides to the topic. Then, the next sentence supporting one side.

15. The correct answer is A. The article talks about a professor's proposition that there are Black mermaids based on African cosmologies, therefore, supporting the possibility that Arial could be Black.

16. The correct answer is D. The article talks about a professor's proposition that there are Black mermaids based on African cosmologies, therefore, supporting the possibility that Arial could be Black. In African cosmologies, "people who were lost to the water could become water spirits."

17. The correct answer is C. Saying that view couldn't be further from truth means that it can possibly be true but not completely true or proven.

18. The correct answer is E. The article shares a professor's opinion on the topic of Ariel being possibly Black based on studies in mermaid mythology related to the Middle Passage, a time period where Africans were enslaved and violently transported across the ocean to North America and the Caribbean, which was a common motif of mermaid legends.

19. The correct answer is B. The article shares a professor's opinion on the topic of Ariel being possibly Black based on studies in mermaid mythology related to the Middle Passage, a time period where Africans were enslaved and violently transported across the ocean to North America and the Caribbean, which was a common motif of mermaid legends.

20. The correct answer is A. The article talks about the facts on whey protein, proven health benefits and risks.

21. The correct answer is C. Whey protein supplementation has been found to help support athletic performance in a literature review and is also promoted for being helpful with diabetes, immune health, asthma, and weight loss.

22. The correct answer is B. Whey protein isn't known to cause harm in most adults when taken in moderate amounts, especially in the protein deficient or those needing more such as athletes, the elderly, or vegetarians.

23. The correct answer is A. A systematic review of both experimental and randomized research studies looked at whey protein and the effect on physical health and showed that ongoing long-term use without the help of a medical or nutrition professional can cause side effects on the kidney and liver.

24. The correct answer is E. Whey protein isn't known to cause harm in most adults when taken in moderate amounts, especially in the protein deficient or those needing more such as athletes, the elderly, or vegetarians. Whey protein is an option worth considering to temporarily supplement your protein intake (unless directed by a physician) and shouldn't take the place of a healthy diet.

25. The correct answer is E. The passage starts with the news on NEDA firing all of its employees and replacing them with an AI-assisted chatbot. Followed by the author's view on the future of AI, laborers, and companies.

26. The correct answer is A. The US-based National Eating Disorders Association (NEDA) is making headlines after firing all its staff and replacing them with an AI-assisted chatbot called Tessa.

27. The correct answer is C. The author shares her opinion on what we expect in the next few years as companies rush to cut costs and replace paid employees with AI.

28. The correct answer is D. As a conclusion, the author mentioned that AI may not end civilizations, but we'll definitely see more companies rushing to adapt to the AI trend and replace paid employees.

29. The correct answer is B. A harbinger is anything that foreshadows a future event omen sign.

30. The correct answer is B. The story mainly talks about Cissa.

31. The correct answer is C. In winter, the days are shorter and the nights longer. Short winter days have long, cold nights.

32. The correct answer is C. This phrase describes how someone grows older.

33. The correct answer is B. A frock is a gown or dress worn by a girl or a woman.

34. The correct answer is A. Puzzling means confusing or baffling.

35. The correct answer is D. The story describes the scenery of a valley in a secluded and mountainous part of Stiria where there is a Golden River, and the land is fertile.

36. The correct answer is E. The clouds were drawn so constantly to the snowy hills, and rested so softly in the circular hollow, that in time of drought and heat, when all country round was burnt up, there was still rain in the little valley; and its crops were so heavy, and its hay so high, and its apples so red, and its grapes so blue, and its wine so rich, and its honey so sweet, that was a marvel to everyone who beheld it, and was commonly called the Treasure Valley.

37. The correct answer is A. The valley never dries up in time of drought and heat because clouds were drawn so constantly to the hills making it rain therefore crops are thriving.

38. The correct answer is D. The valley never dries up in time of drought and heat because clouds were drawn so constantly to the hills making it rain therefore crops are thriving.

39. The correct answer is B. When the sun had set to everything else, and all below was darkness, his beams still shone full upon this waterfall, so that it looked like a shower of gold.

40. The correct answer is B. Populous means full of residents or inhabitants, as a region; heavily populated.

Section 4

1. A	11. E	21. B	31. C	41. D	51. B
2. B	12. A	22. A	32. A	42. A	52. C
3. C	13. C	23. D	33. B	43. C	53. A
4. D	14. D	24. D	34. B	44. C	54. C
5. B	15. B	25. C	35. D	45. B	55. C
6. C	16. B	26. E	36. C	46. A	56. D
7. A	17. C	27. B	37. A	47. D	57. A
8. D	18. D	28. A	38. A	48. A	58. A
9. D	19. E	29. A	39. B	49. C	59. B
10. A	20. E	30. C	40. C	50. B	60. C

1. The correct answer is A. Amiable means having or showing pleasant, good-natured personal qualities.

2. The correct answer is B. Aloof means reserved or reticent; indifferent; disinterested.

3. The correct answer is C. Apathetic means not interested or concerned; indifferent or unresponsive.

4. The correct answer is D. To abduct means to carry off or lead away (a person) illegally and in secret or by force. Synonyms are, to kidnap, seize, or snatch.

5. The correct answer is B. Absurd means inconsistent with reason or logic or common sense.

6. The correct answer is C. To acclaim means to welcome or salute with shouts or sounds of joy and approval; applaud.

7. The correct answer is A. An adage is a traditional saying expressing a common experience or observation; proverb.

8. The correct answer is D. To suspend is to suspend the meeting of (a club, legislature, committee, etc.) to a future time, another place, or indefinitely.

9. The correct answer is D. To admonish is to reprove or scold, especially in a mild and good-willed manner.

10. The correct answer is A. An adversary is a person, group, or force that opposes or attacks; opponent; enemy; foe.

11. The correct answer is E. Boisterous means rough and noisy; noisily jolly or rowdy; clamorous; unrestrained.

12. The correct answer is A. Brevity means shortness of time or duration; briefness.

13. The correct answer is C. Bliss means supreme happiness; utter joy or contentment.

14. The correct answer is D. Blunt means having an obtuse, thick, or dull edge or point; rounded; not sharp. It can also be used as abruptly plain and direct in address or manner, without attempting to be tactful.

15. The correct answer is B. Bleak means without hope or encouragement; depressing; dreary.

16. The correct answer is B. To blunder means to move or act blindly, stupidly, or without direction or steady guidance.

17. The correct answer is C. Boorish means of or like a boor; unmannered; crude; insensitive.

18. The correct answer is D. To banter means to tease; exchange of light, playful, teasing remarks; good-natured raillery.

19. The correct answer is E. Brisk means quick and active; lively.

20. The correct answer is E. Brink means any extreme edge; verge.

21. The correct answer is B. A cache is a hiding place, especially one in the ground, for ammunition, food, treasures.

22. The correct answer is A. To coax means to attempt to influence by gentle persuasion, flattery, etc.; cajole.

23. The correct answer is D. Capricious is subject to, led by, or indicative of a sudden, odd notion or unpredictable change; erratic.

24. The correct answer is D. To cascade means to fall in or like a cascade.

25. The correct answer is C. To collide means to strike one another or one against the other with a forceful impact; come into violent contact; crash.

26. The correct answer is E. To compel means to force or drive, especially to a course of action.

27. The correct answer is B. To condone means to disregard or overlook (something illegal, objectionable, or the like).

28. The correct answer is A. To contemplate means to consider thoroughly; think fully or deeply about.

29. The correct answer is A. To contend means to strive in rivalry; compete; vie.

30. The correct answer is C. To convene means to come together or assemble, usually for some public purpose.

31. The correct answer is C. To loiter means to pass (time) in an idle or aimless manner.

32. The correct answer is A. Debris is the remains of anything broken down or destroyed; ruins; rubble.

33. The correct answer is B. Decade is a period of 10 years which in this sentence also meant a long time.

34. The correct answer is B. To delude means to mislead the mind or judgment of; deceive.

35. The correct answer is D. Deficit means a disadvantage, impairment, or handicap.

36. The correct answer is C. Dehydration means an abnormal loss of water from the body, especially from illness or physical exertion.

37. The correct answer is A. Despicable means deserving to be despised, or regarded with distaste, disgust, or disdain; contemptible.

38. The correct answer is A. To diminish means to make or cause to seem smaller, less, less important, etc.; lessen; reduce.

39. The correct answer is B. To disclaim means to deny or repudiate interest in or connection with; disavow; disown.

40. The correct answer is C. Discourse means communication of thought by words; talk; conversation.

41. The correct answer is D. Unfortunate means unfavorable or inauspicious. Dismal means causing gloom or dejection; gloomy; dreary; cheerless; melancholy. In this sentence, it was unfortunate for their team to have a game on such a dismal weather.

42. The correct answer is A. Dispute means a disagreement, argument, or debate.

43. The correct answer is C. To forbid means to prohibit (something); make a rule or law against. To disseminate means to scatter or spread widely, as though sowing seed; promulgate extensively; broadcast; disperse.

44. The correct answer is C. To divert means to turn aside or from a path or course; deflect.

45. The correct answer is B. Ecstatic means subject to or in a state of ecstasy; full of joy; rapturous.

46. The correct answer is A. Elusive means cleverly or skillfully evasive.

47. The correct answer is D. To embellish means to beautify by or as if by ornamentation; ornament; adorn. Embellished is an adjective which means adorned, fancy, and elaborate.

48. The correct answer is A. To enact means to represent on or as on the stage; act the part of.

49. The correct answer is C. To encompass means to include comprehensively.

50. The correct answer is B. Enigma means a puzzling or inexplicable occurrence or situation. Distress means great pain, anxiety, or sorrow; acute physical or mental suffering; affliction; trouble.

51. The correct answer is B. The words have a specific–general category relationship. Coffee is a beverage, while salt is a seasoning.

52. The correct answer is C. The words have an object–source of power relationship. A car needs fuel to run as a cellphone needs battery to function.

53. The correct answer is A. The words have an object–purpose relationship. Soap is used to lather on the body as shampoo is used to clean the hair.

54. The correct answer is C. The words are antonyms. The opposite of accept is reject as the opposite of send is to receive.

55. The correct answer is C. The words have an object–purpose relationship. You use a towel to dry something wet as you use a kettle to boil water or tea.

56. The correct answer is D. The words have a specific–general category relationship. A train is a vehicle as a table is a furniture.

57. The correct answer is A. The words have an object–purpose relationship. Fire is used to produce heat as ice is used to keep something cold.

58. The correct answer is A. The words have an animal–action relationship. Fishes swim as horses gallop.

59. The correct answer is B. Something that is tiny is small. Something that is giant is large.

60. The correct answer is C. Something that is cut is made short. Something that is extended is prolonged.

Section 5

1. A	6. B	11. E	16. E	21. C
2. E	7. D	12. A	17. C	22. D
3. C	8. C	13. C	18. A	23. A
4. A	9. C	14. D	19. D	24. B
5. E	10. A	15. B	20. B	25. E

1. **Answer: A**

    The factors of 36 are (1,36), (2,18), (3,12), (4,9), (6,6). (6,6) will count as 1 since it's the same number. There will be a total of 9 factors, hence the answer is A.

2. **Answer: E**

    The total measure of the angles of a pentagon is 540° (based on 180° $(n - 2)$, where n is the number of angles. If the measures of the angles form an arithmetic sequence, the angles will be increasing by some common difference (d): 70, 70 + d, 70 + 2d, 70 + 3d, 70 + 4d. With this pattern, we can get the value of the difference (d): 70 + 70 + d + 70 + 2d + 70 + 3d + 70 + 4d = 540 ➡ 10d + 350 = 540 ➡ 10d = 190 ➡ d = 19. The largest angle is 70 + 4d, substitute d with 19: 70 + 4(19) = 70 + 76 = 146. The largest angle is 146°, hence the answer is E.

3. **Answer: C**

    To get the reciprocal, we need to convert the decimals to fractions: $\frac{2}{10}$ and $\frac{9}{10}$. The reciprocals of these are $\frac{10}{2}$ and $\frac{10}{9}$. Let's add: $\frac{10}{2} + \frac{10}{9} = \frac{90+20}{18} = \frac{110}{18} = 6\frac{1}{9}$. The answer is C.

4. **Answer: A**

    Since E is the midpoint of AB, we can add point F that could be the midpoint of DC. We have now four triangles: DAE, EFD, CBE, and EFC. By adding the midpoint F, the areas of these four triangles will be equal. Let x be the area of one of the triangles: 4x = 240 ➡ x = 60. The shaded part consists of two triangles, so we will multiply the value of x by 2, which will result in 120 cm², hence the answer is A.

5. **Answer: E**

    There's not enough data to get the value of x, hence the answer is E.

6. **Answer: B**

    Let x be the first odd integer, x + 2 be the second odd integer, and x + 4 be the third odd integer. Add: x + x + 2 + x + 4 = 477 ➡ 3x + 6 = 477 ➡ 3x = 471 ➡ x = 157. The smallest integer is 157, while the largest integer is 157 + 4 = 161. Add the two integers: 157 + 161 = 318. The sum is 318, hence the answer is B.

7. **Answer: D**

    Let's divide: 67,234 ÷ 392 = 171.52. Among the choices, option D is the closest, hence the answer is D.

8. **Answer: C**

   Subtract: $(8x - 5y + 2z) - (3x + 2y - 6z) = 8x - 5y + 2z - 3x - 2y + 6z = 5x - 7y + 8z$. The answer is C.

9. **Answer: C**

   To change a mixed fraction to its improper fraction, first copy the denominator, next multiply the denominator to the whole number, and lastly add the product of the denominator and the whole number to the numerator. $2\frac{11}{19}$ will be $\frac{49}{19}$. The new numerator will be 49, hence the answer is C.

10. **Answer: A**

    Let $1.5x$ be the total number of kilograms of oats and $2.5x$ be the total number of kilograms of grass. $1.5x + 2.5x = 20 \Rightarrow 4x = 20 \Rightarrow x = 5$. Substitute: $2.5x = 2.5(5) = 12.5$. The cow ate a total of 12.5 kg of grass, hence the answer is A.

11. **Answer: E**

    Let's add: $52.64 + 37.03 + 84.75 = 174.42$. Lisa spent \$174.42, hence the answer is E.

12. **Answer: A**

    To get the surface area of a cube, use the formula $SA = 6s^2 = 6(6^2) = 216$. The surface area is 216 in², hence the answer is A.

13. **Answer: C**

    To get the length of the other leg, we can use the Pythagorean theorem: $c^2 = a^2 + b^2 \Rightarrow 13^2 = 12^2 + b^2 \Rightarrow 169 = 144 + b^2 \Rightarrow b^2 = 25 \Rightarrow b = 5$. The other leg measures 5 m, hence the answer is C.

14. **Answer: D**

    The y-intercept is the point at which the graph crosses the y-axis. At this point, the x-coordinate is 0, so substitute 0 for x in the equation: $y = 5(x - 1)^2 + 2(x - 3) \Rightarrow y = 5(0 - 1)^2 + 2(0 - 3) \Rightarrow y = 5(-1)^2 + 2(-3) \Rightarrow y = 5 - 6 \Rightarrow y = -1$. The y-intercept is point $(0, -1)$, hence the answer is D.

15. **Answer: B**

    Subtract the books that were borrowed for June and March: $250 - 102 = 148$. The difference is 148 books, hence the answer is B.

16. **Answer: E**

    The given data is for the year 2022 and what Suzanne needs is the data for the year 2023, hence the answer is E.

17. **Answer: C**

    The amount of money for x bookshelf is $170x$; the total cost of all the bookshelves is $170x + 350$; the total cost, in dollar, per bookshelf will be $\frac{total\ cost\ of\ all\ bookshelves}{total\ number\ of\ bookshelves} = \frac{170x + 350}{x}$. The answer is C.

18. Answer: A

The formula to get the perimeter of a pentagon is $P = 5s$. We can use this formula to get the length of one side. $24 = 5s \Rightarrow s = 4.8$ m. Now that we have the length of one side, convert the result to mm: $4.8 \times 1000 = 4,800$ mm. The answer is A.

19. Answer: D

The formula to get the perimeter of a square is $P = 4s = 4(x + 8) = 4x + 32$. The answer is D.

20. Answer: B

The equation of a circle on a coordinate plane is $x^2 + y^2 = r^2$, where r is the radius. Let's get the square root of 324 to get the radius: $\sqrt{324} = 18$. Now that we have the radius, we can solve for the circumference: $C = 2\pi r = 2\pi (18) = 36\pi$. The circumference is 36π, hence the answer is B.

21. Answer: C

The equation of a circle on a coordinate plane is $x^2 + y^2 = r^2$, where r is the radius. Let's get the square root of 576 to get the radius: $\sqrt{576} = 24$. Now that we have the radius, we can solve for the circumference: $C = 2\pi r = 2\pi (24) = 48\pi$. The circumference is 48π, hence the answer is C.

22. Answer: D

The equation of a circle on a coordinate plane is $x^2 + y^2 = r^2$, where r is the radius. To get the area of a circle, use the formula $A = \pi r^2 = 45\pi$. The area is 45π, hence the answer is D.

23. Answer: A

Let's get the total number of marbles in the jar: $5 + 7 + 11 = 23$. There are five blue marbles, so the probability of Ysabel getting a blue marble will be $\dfrac{5}{23}$, hence the answer is A.

24. Answer: B

To get the volume of the sphere, use the formula $V = \dfrac{4}{3}\pi r^3 \Rightarrow 250 = \dfrac{4}{3}\pi r^3 \Rightarrow r^3 = \dfrac{3 \times 250}{4\pi} \Rightarrow r = 3.91$. the diameter is $2r = 2(3.91) = 7.82$ in, hence the answer is B.

25. Answer: E

Since this reasoning is valid regardless of the actual score, let's assume that Quincy's score is 100. Nathan who outscored Quincy by 21 points will have 121 points. Troy who outscored Nathan by 17 points will have 138 points. Lilian who outscored Nathan by 49 points will have 170 points. Cass will have 147 points. This will make the order from highest to lowest: Lilian, Cass, Troy, Nathan, Quincy. The third highest will be Troy, hence the answer is E.

SSAT Upper Level Exam 2

SECTION 1

WRITING SAMPLE

Time—25 minutes

Directions: Using two sheets of lined theme paper, plan and write an essay on the topic assigned below. DO NOT WRITE ON ANOTHER TOPIC. AN ESSAY ON ANOTHER TOPIC IS NOT ACCEPTABLE.

Topic: The impact of technology to our daily lives.

Directions: How has technology affected your daily life? Use reasons and specific examples to support your answer.

_____

_____

_____

_____

_____

_____

_____

_____

_____

_____

_____

_____

_____

_____

_____

_____

_____

_____

SECTION 2

QUANTITATIVE MATH

Time—30 minutes

25 Questions

Directions: Any figures that accompany questions in this section may be assumed to be drawn as accurately as possible EXCEPT when it is stated that a particular figure is not drawn to scale. Letters such as x, y, and n stand for real numbers.

Each question consists of a word problem followed by five answer choices. You may write in your text booklet; however, you may also be able to solve many of these problems in your head. Next, take a look at the five answer choices and select the best one.

Example

5,413 – 4,827 =

(A) 586
(B) 596
(C) 696
(D) 1,586
(E) 1,686

Answer

● Ⓑ Ⓒ Ⓓ Ⓔ

The correct answer to this question is lettered A, so space A is marked.

1. The length of a rectangle is three times its width. If the perimeter of the rectangle is 160 mm, what is the area of the rectangle?

   (A) 1000 mm² (B) 100 mm² (C) 120 mm² (D) 1200 mm² (E) 1500 mm²

2. What would be the surface area, in square inches, of a cube if the length of one side is 12.5 in?

   (A) 937.5 in² (B) 935.7 in² (C) 973.5 in² (D) 975.3 in² (E) 939 in²

3. A pair of shoes normally sells for $189.00, but because of the holidays, it was put on sale for 55% off. What would be the new cost of the shoes?

   (A) $58.05 (B) $58.50 (C) $85.05 (D) $85.50 (E) $103.95

4. Mathilda just received her paycheck. If 15% of her salary was deducted for taxes and 3% for insurance, what is the total percentage taken out of her paycheck?

   (A) 20% (B) 82% (C) 18% (D) 16% (E) 8%

5. What is the sum of the exterior angles of an equilateral triangle?

   (A) 180° (B) 360° (C) 60° (D) 240° (E) 300°

6. Andrew plans to give a planner to each of his 25 new employees as a welcome gift. Five planners come in a box. How many boxes of planners must he buy?

   (A) 5 (B) 2 (C) 7 (D) 11 (E) 6

7. Lucy receives a standard rate of $14 for every flower bouquet she assembles. When she makes more than 12 bouquets in a week, Lucy will be paid an additional $17.50 per bouquet for every bouquet after the 12th one she assembles. How much will be her salary during a week in which she assembles 22 flower bouquets?

   (A) $334.00 (B) $433.00 (C) $334.50 (D) $343.50 (E) $343.00

8. The average length of four female hamsters is 5.7 in, and the average length of seven male hamsters is 6.3 in. What is the average length, in inches, of all eleven hamsters?

   (A) 6.8 in (B) 6.08 in (C) 6.81 in (D) 8.06 in (E) 8.6 in

9. A survey was conducted among St. Mont High School students. With the data collected, it was found out that each of 200 respondents uses a smartphone, a laptop, or both for their online classes. If 150 of these students uses smartphones and 75 of them uses laptops, how many students use both smartphone and laptop?

   (A) 50 (B) 150 (C) 75 (D) 25 (E) 100

10. Mr. Clint wanted to buy a sofa for his new house. It was on sale for $2250. He was offered two options to pay for it: pay the entire amount in one payment with cash, or pay $1000 as a down payment and $80 per month for two full years in a financial plan. If Mr. Clint chooses the financial plan, how much more would he pay?

    (A) $670 (B) $760 (C) $706 (D) $607 (E) $700

11. What is the average of $\frac{15}{3}$ and 45.8?

    (A) 24.5 (B) 42.5 (C) 45.2 (D) 2.54 (E) 25.4

12. The sum of five times a number and 72 is 247. What is the number?

    (A) 70 (B) 53 (C) 35 (D) 40 (E) 65

13. If two numbers, K and L, have an average of 60, $K - L \neq 0$ and $K < L$, which must be true?

    (A) $K - L = 30$ (B) $K + L = 60$ (C) $K = 20$ and $L = 40$ (D) $60 - K = L - 80$ (E) none of the above

14. When school started, Ken gave Sabrina 40% of his anime card collection. Seeing that Sabrina was eager to play with it, he gave 40% of the remaining cards in his collection to her the following day. What percent does Ken still have out of his original collection?

(A) 25% (B) 42% (C) 30% (D) 20% (E) 36%

15. Farrah bought a ticket to a concert of a famous boy band. But something came up with her work and she won't be able to attend to it. She is planning to sell her concert ticket for 57% of the original price. If Farrah paid $58.94 for the ticket, approximately how much will she sell her ticket for?

(A) $33.30 (B) $33.60 (C) $36.30 (D) $36.60 (E) $35.00

16. The volume of a sphere is 1000 in³. What is the diameter of the sphere?

(A) 14.2 in (B) 13.14 in (C) 12.4 in (D) 11.12 in (E) 15.5 in

17. A regular hexagon has perimeter 45 ft. What would be the length of each side in inches?

(A) 7.5 ft (B) 8.5 ft (C) 9 ft (D) 6.3 ft (E) 8 ft

18. In a jar, there are 7 blue marbles, 9 red marbles, 4 yellow marbles. If Ross reaches his hand in the jar and grabs one marble, what is the probability he will pick up a blue marble?

(A) 35% (B) 40% (C) 30% (D) 42% (E) 32%

19. If the sum of the smallest and largest of three consecutive even numbers is 152, what is the value of the second largest number?

(A) 74 (B) 78 (C) 76 (D) 80 (E) 72

20. A line can be represented by $2x + 4y = 8$. What is the slope of the line that is perpendicular to it?

(A) $-\dfrac{1}{2}$ (B) 2 (C) $\dfrac{1}{2}$ (D) -2 (E) $-\dfrac{1}{4}$

21. In the year 2015, 29% of the company sales were in cosmetics. The table below shows how cosmetics sale has changed for the company over the years. Find the percentage of cosmetics sold in 2020.

Years	Change
2015–2016	+3%
2016–2017	–1%
2017–2018	–1%
2018–2019	+4%
2019–2020	+7%

(A) 29% (B) 35% (C) 48% (D) 42% (E) 39%

22. Marissa is participating in a marathon for a fundraising charity. Her parents are going to contribute $2.00 after she runs one mile, $4.00 after she runs two miles, and $6.00 after she runs three miles. If her parents continue to donate money in this manner, how much money will Marissa's parents contribute to her charity if Marissa runs 18 miles?

(A) $300   (B) $342   (C) $452   (D) $332   (E) $406

23. The perimeter of an equilateral triangle is equal to the half of the perimeter of a square. If the length of the side of the square is 12 cm, what is the length of a side of the triangle?

(A) 12 cm   (B) 10 cm   (C) 14 cm   (D) 8 cm   (E) 6 cm

24. A fair coin is tossed nine times. Each toss comes up heads. What is the probability that the coin will come up heads a tenth time?

(A) $\dfrac{1}{2}$ (B) $\dfrac{9}{10}$ (C) $\dfrac{1}{5}$ (D) $\dfrac{3}{4}$ (E) $\dfrac{3}{5}$

25. Mr. Rivera is going to apply a fertilizer to his rectangular farm which has a dimension of 350 ft by 150 ft. Every pound of the fertilizer that he is going to use is sufficient for 60 sq ft. If the fertilizer costs $3.70 per pound, how much should he spend to fertilize his farm?

(A) $3,732.50   (B) $3,723.50   (C) $3,237.50   (D) $3,327.50   (E) $3,273.50

READING COMPREHENSION

Time—40 minutes

40 Questions

Directions: This section contains seven short reading passages. Each passage is followed by several questions based on its content. Answer the questions following the passage on the basis of what is stated or implied in that passage. You may write in your test booklet.

Passage 1

In response to those threats the Hawaii Legislature made the state the first in the nation to declare a climate emergency in 2021, <u>asserting</u> that the right to a healthy environment is a basic human right, as proclaimed decades earlier in the state constitution.

That human rights framing has since made its way to the Hawaii Supreme Court.

In a recent case that grabbed headlines, owners of a proposed Hu Honua biomass plant wanted to burn eucalyptus trees and other invasive species to generate power to be sold to the Hawaii Electric Co. grid. In response to the state's estimate that burning the biomass would generate some 8 million metric tons of carbon over its 30-year lifespan, the facility owners promised to plant enough trees – estimated at 3.1 million – to offset its emissions, making the plan carbon-neutral or even carbon-negative.

That promise wasn't sufficient for the court, with justices on March 13 unanimously rejecting the plan.

"Hawaii is in a climate emergency and the State bears a constitutional duty to limit greenhouse gas emissions to prevent additional global warming," wrote then-Hawaii Supreme Court Justice Michael D. Wilson, who argued that approval of the agreement would "violate the people of Hawaii's right to a life-sustaining climate system." He added that climate change is "a human rights issue at its core," and it disproportionately harms youth, future generations and Native peoples.

from Hawaii Tackles Climate Change With a Human Rights Focus by *Nancy Cook Lauer, US News*

1. The passage is mainly about the _____.

(A) the effects of carbon monoxide emission to the ozone

(B) how climate change has affected the world

(C) how Hawaii has been staying true to the right to a healthy environment as proven by the rejection to the biomass plant's proposal

(D) proposal to remove the right to a healthy environment to pave way to more businesses

(E) approval of the biomass plant to help Hawaii's economy in lieu of progress

2. What state was the topic of the passage?

   (A) Hawaii   (B) New York   (C) New Jersey   (D) Honolulu   (E) all of the United States

3. How is Hawaii different from other states in relation to climate change?

   (A) the only state that has zero carbon emissions

   (B) the first in the nation to declare that the right to a healthy environment is a basic human right

   (C) the only state that conducts carbon monoxide emission testing in vehicles

   (D) the only state that bans burning of fossil fuels

   (E) the only state that protects its forests

4. What motivated the state to amend the constitution to include the right to a healthy environment?

   (A) just for the influence

   (B) prevent additional global warming and protect the youth and future generations

   (C) prevent any more businesses from emerging and taking over opportunities from the locals

   (D) to encourage tourism

   (E) not explained in the passage

5. What is the best reaction after reading the passage?

   (A) devastated that not all nations have this amendment

   (B) disappointed that the biomass plant was rejected

   (C) saddened by the approval of burning trees

   (D) hopeful that the rest of the states will follow Hawaii as an example

   (E) dismayed that planting 3.1 million trees was rejected

6. What does "asserting" mean?

   (A) to state that (something declared or believed to be true) is not true

   (B) to refuse to agree or accede to

   (C) to withhold the possession, use, or enjoyment of

   (D) to maintain or defend (claims, rights, etc.)

   (E) to withhold (someone) from accessibility to a visitor

7. What is the purpose of the article?

   (A) to give information on Hawaii's movement against climate change

   (B) to disagree with Hawaii's decision to reject the biomass plant

   (C) to persuade people to travel to Hawaii

   (D) to educate people on the advantages of biomass plants to the economy

   (E) to identify top reasons of climate change

Passage 2

For high school students or graduates considering a gap year, the options are plentiful and include structured programs or self-guided exploration.

The Gap Year Association, which accredits numerous programs, lists experiences with a focus on ecology, animal welfare and conservation, language studies, coding, cultural immersion and a variety of other topics.

Another option is AmeriCorps, which offers a number of service programs throughout the country for those 18 or older. Students who participate are eligible for benefits such as a living allowance and an education award that can be used to pay off loans or put toward future tuition.

Students may also elect to work during a gap year, either to make money for college or to earn college credit through an internship.

"The best gap years tend to be the ones that push students to think about who they are and their role in the world," says Joe O'Shea, associate provost and dean of undergraduate studies at Florida State University and author of "Gap Year: How Delaying College Changes People in Ways the World Needs."

O'Shea says a gap year can help motivate and inspire students and better prepare them for college. He notes that the "natural break" between high school and college is an ideal time for students to "pause and reflect" and explore options before their studies begin.

"Often you see students who struggle in higher education because they don't have a sense of purpose and direction," O'Shea says. "Gap years – because they give students a broader sense of the world and their place in it and how they can contribute – help to supply and empower students with the kind of motivation and purpose that can animate their entire college experience."

from How a Gap Year Prepares Students for College by *Cole Claybourn, US News*

8. The passage is mainly about _____.

   (A) program to encourage students to delay going to college

   (B) best universities to apply to after graduating high school

   (C) gap year and the programs and options available for those who undergo it

   (D) most wanted college degrees that will ensure a brighter future

   (E) best things to do after high school instead of going to college

9. What is a gap year?

   (A) a vacation to take the stress away

   (B) a year before graduating high school in preparation for college

   (C) delaying or taking a break after high school graduation before entering college

   (D) a prerequisite year to study your major in advance before college

   (E) the first year of college

10. What are the objectives of a gap year?

    (A) help motivate and inspire students

    (B) better prepare graduates for college

    (C) they may elect to work to make money for college or earn college credit

    (D) that push students to think about who they are and their role in the world

    (E) all of the above

11. How does one decide if they need a gap year?

    (A) if they feel exhausted from studying

    (B) options are plentiful and include structured programs or self-guided exploration

    (C) when they can't pass the college entrance exams

    (D) if they graduate in the middle of the school year

    (E) when location is an issue

12. How does the Gap Year Association support the students?

    (A) they offer student loans

    (B) they offer part-time jobs so the students can earn money

    (C) through numerous programs, lists experiences with a focus on a variety of topics

    (D) they have a cram school to get them prepared for the entrance exams

    (E) they are a rehabilitation center to destress

13. Which words means similar to "accredit"?

    (A) certify   (B) deny   (C) disapprove   (D) reject   (E) refuse

Passage 3

So, the overcrowded boat was left in the high seas without a captain and with a malfunctioning engine, making steering nearly impossible, according to transcripts of distress <u>purportedly</u> received by Alarm Phone. Water flooded the lower deck and people rushed to the top, drenched and facing the brunt of the chilling wind.

"The children shiver with cold," a woman said at around 8 p.m. As the hours passed, the boat continued to drift without a rescue attempt being launched.

When NBC News requested comment on the case, the Armed Forces of Malta said in a statement: "Written communication received by the AFM from the ship captain providing duty of care confirms that no rescue was requested by the people on board." It was not clear which ship captain the statement was referring to, and representatives from Malta did not respond to several requests for follow-up comment.

Malta's, FMT URLA's and Pericles' responses fell far short of what was required of them, according to Velasco.

"Supplying fresh water or offering fuel in those circumstances is clearly insufficient and inadequate," she said.

Eventually, on April 12, when the ship drifted into Italian waters, that country's coast guard dispatched rescue vessels and brought the starving migrants to their shores.

from Dangerously overcrowded ship drifted in Mediterranean for days without being rescued by *Mithil Aggarwal, NBC News*

14. What is the passage about?

(A) about the best place to get stranded in a ship

(B) about the ideal number of passengers a ship can hold

(C) about an overcrowded ship not being rescued for days

(D) advertisement to buy cruise tickets

(E) discouraging people to board a ship

15. What caused the delay in rescue?

(A) no equipment

(B) the storm

(C) lack of proper communication

(D) there was not enough manpower

(E) the ship was unknown

16. What happened to the boat and its passengers in the end?

(A) got stranded in the Atlantic

(B) they went missing and never found

(C) Italy's coast guard dispatched rescue vessels

(D) the ship sunk

(E) the passengers rode the ship's lifeboats and sailed to a nearby island

17. Which sentence uses the word "purportedly" correctly?

(A) the photos purportedly show the celebrity with a new boyfriend

(B) there was not purportedly schedule

(C) she cheered purportedly

(D) he purportedly ended his class

(E) yours purportedly, Emma

18. Which best describes the overall mood of the article?

(A) cheerful   (B) suspenseful   (C) joyous   (D) triumphant   (E) celebratory

19. What is the meaning of the word "purportedly"?

(A) in accordance with fact or truth

(B) according to what is or has been claimed

(C) legitimately

(D) to the fullest extent or degree

(E) sincerely

Passage 4

Headlines warning of new Covid variants; unseasonal <u>surges</u> of flu, RSV and human metapneumovirus; and unusual symptoms stemming from viruses that usually cause cold-like symptoms, including adenovirus and enterovirus, have made many of us hyper aware of the germs that make us sick.

But is the extra attention and worry over what exactly is causing your stuffy nose or cough necessary?

Put simply, no, experts say, but there are some exceptions for people with weakened immune systems.

"During the pandemic, we generally ran every test available because we wanted to know if it was Covid or if there was an alternative diagnosis, but this over-testing has carried into this post-Covid era," said Dr. Chris Chao, an urgent care physician at WakeMed Health & Hospitals in Raleigh, North Carolina, and president of the College of Urgent Care Medicine. "People want to know what's wrong with them and saying it's just a virus is not good enough anymore. Everyone who comes in with a sore throat now wants a strep, flu and Covid test, but in most cases none of that's really indicated."

Respiratory viral panels can detect more than a dozen viruses at once, including influenza and SARS-CoV-2, the virus that causes Covid, as well as a number of viruses that cause colds: RSV, adenovirus, rhinovirus, enterovirus and HMPV.

However, for healthy people with mild cold symptoms, doctors say these tests are not worth the cost because treatment—hydration, rest, cough suppressants if needed—is the same for most viruses. (Viral infections are not treatable with antibiotics.)

from What happened to the common cold? Post-Covid, it feels like every sniffle needs a name. by *Katie Camero, NBC News*

20. What is the main topic of the article?

   (A) to educate people that influenza virus continues to evolve

   (B) to encourage people to always ask for all available tests to ensure correct diagnosis

   (C) to inform people what are the best hospitals to go to when they are sick

   (D) to educate people that over-testing is not necessary post COVID

   (E) to convince people not to see doctors when they only have flu symptoms

21. After reading the passage, which best concludes it?

   (A) always visit the largest hospitals when you have flu symptoms as they are continuously evolving

   (B) do not go seeing doctors when you only have the common flu symptoms

   (C) over-testing is necessary even post COVID to endure diagnosis and monitor new virus strains

   (D) extra attention, worry over what is causing your flu symptoms, and over-testing are not necessary unless you have a weak immune system

   (E) whether you are immune-deprived or healthy, you do not need extra care when you have flu symptoms

22. When are these tests not necessary?

   (A) for healthy people with mild cold symptoms

   (B) for people who are already on multiple medications

   (C) for people taking supplements

   (D) for people at the end of their life

   (E) for ages 12–34

23. What is the treatment for most viruses?

   (A) *hydration* and rest

   (B) cough suppressants if needed

   (C) both A and B

   (D) switching to vegan diet

   (E) antibiotics

24. What is the meaning of the word "surge"?

(A) a twilled worsted or woolen fabric

(B) a physician who specializes in surgery

(C) a sudden, strong increase

(D) the swell of the sea that breaks upon a shore

(E) to search haphazardly, as for information on a computer network

Passage 5

I am Buffalo Bill's horse. I have spent my life under his saddle—with him in it, too, and he is good for two hundred pounds, without his clothes; and there is no telling how much he does weigh when he is out on the war-path and has his batteries belted on. He is over six feet, is young, hasn't an ounce of waste flesh, is straight, graceful, springy in his motions, quick as a cat, and has a handsome face, and black hair dangling down on his shoulders, and is beautiful to look at; and nobody is braver than he is, and nobody is stronger, except myself. Yes, a person that doubts that he is fine to see should see him in his beaded buckskins, on my back and his rifle peeping above his shoulder, chasing a hostile trail, with me going like the wind and his hair streaming out behind from the shelter of his broad slouch. Yes, he is a sight to look at then—and I'm part of it myself.

I am his favorite horse, out of the dozens. Big as he is, I have carried him eighty-one miles between nightfall and sunrise on the scout; and I am a good for fifty, day in and day out, and all the time. I am not large, but I am built on a business basis.

from A Horse's Tale by *Mark Twain*

25. What is the passage about?

(A) about how good-looking Buffalo Bill is

(B) about Buffalo Bill's horse and his reflection of himself

(C) about horses used for battle

(D) about the mode of transportation back in the days

(E) about what kind of horses were chosen for rangers

26. Which best describes the speaker of the passage?

(A) humble and quiet

(B) proud and confident

(C) sad and lonely

(D) hopeful and hard-working

(E) creepy and dangerous

27. Who is the speaker of the passage?

    (A) Buffalo Bill (B) a passerby (C) Buffalo bill's horse (D) the author (E) the reader

28. Which best implies what occupation does Buffalo Bill have?

    (A) a ranger (B) a prince (C) a knight in the castle (D) a teacher (E) a priest

29. What does "springy" mean?

    (A) conceitedly assertive and dogmatic in one's opinions

    (B) anything that foreshadows a future event

    (C) characterized by spring or elasticity; flexible

    (D) nearness in space, position, degree, or relation

    (E) something that happens as a consequence

Passage 6

The express from Columbia was due. It was almost nine o'clock on Tuesday night, the 31st of August 1886. It had been a hot day, sultry toward the night, and the loungers at the Summerville station were divided between pitying and envying neighbors on the excursion train. In such weather, home seems either the most intolerable or the most comfortable place in the world. It had not rained for six weeks, and South Carolina panted.

There was a larger crowd than usual at the little station to see the Columbia excursionists come in. The enterprise of the Summerville merchant who placarded the pine-trees of this forest village with legends to the effect that his ice-cream would be found "Opp. the depot," was well rewarded that scorching night. The streets thronged—if Summerville streets can ever be said to throng—with warm and thirsty loungers of both sexes and color. South Carolinians though they were, they objected to the heat of the sun.

from A Lost Hero by *Elizabeth Stuart Phelps*

30. What vehicle is referred to as the express?

    (A) horse carriage (B) bike (C) train (D) sports car (E) wagon

31. What season was described in the passage?

    (A) winter (B) snowy (C) summer (D) autumn (E) fall

32. Which best describes how the people felt according to the passage?

    (A) chilly (B) frigid (C) sweltering (D) freezing (E) fresh

33. What does "excursionist" mean?

(A) a person who captured criminals

(B) a traveler

(C) in charge of executions

(D) a gymnast

(E) a driver

34. Which word best describes how the ice-cream business of the merchant went during that day in the passage?

(A) successful   (B) hopeless   (C) unfortunate   (D) defeated   (E) unprofitable

Passage 7

"Once upon a time"

"Is it a fairy story?" questioned Alice and Ella both in a breath.

"Well, one kind of a fairy story; and you may tell me the fairy's name, if you can, when I have finished"; and then she commenced again:

"Once upon a time, there was a great commotion in the forest; the leaves began to peep out of their dark winter blankets and don their spring dresses."

"Miss Maple shook out the folds of her crimson satin, and at once all the honeybees came to do her homage. Mr. Beech dressed himself in a suit glossy green, and it became the fashion; and all the gentlemen who wanted to move in the 'first circles' followed his example."

"Presently a little violet opened her blue eyes and smiled to see how fine her stately neighbors were looking, as she was gazing around, she spied two bright green leaves that were strangers in that neighborhood."

"'What might I call you?' asked the violet, with a little bend of the head, and a sweet smile."

"My name is Oak, and I'm called the 'King of the Forest,'" he answered, trying to stretch up a little, so as to get sight of a lady-bug who was singing softly to herself under a toad-stool umbrella.

"'Ha! ha! a king! a king!' cried Miss Maple, and she laughed until some of the crimson blossoms with which she had decked her head fell at the feet of the self-styled monarch."

"Then Mr. Beech cast his eyes down, and with the utmost disdain exclaimed:"

"'A beautiful monarch, truly, with your two leaves and not a sign of a crown!"

"Just then a bright little fairy hopped out of a forget-me-not, and coming up close to the despondent oak, whispered softly:"

"'Take heart, little oak! take heart! Don't you know that merit is seldom appreciated unless accompanied by show? So, mind nothing about this ridicule; but make friends of the sun and dew, and don't try to stretch up your head until your feet are firmly set, and be modest, retiring, and generous, and the time will come when you will be far above all these silly people both in position and fame.'"

from Aunt Eunice's fairy Story *by Marcia Melissa Bassett Goodwin*

35. What is the story about?

(A) about Tinkerbell and her friends

(B) about the diverse species of trees in the nearby forest

(C) about the might Maple Tree

(D) about Aunt Eunice's story of the little Oak and the fairy

(E) about her adventures as a little girl

36. Which feeling best implies how the sisters felt about their Aunt Eunice's story?

(A) terrified   (B) melancholic   (C) sad   (D) bored   (E) excited

37. Which best describes the scenery from the story?

(A) full and vibrant   (B) gray and gloomy   (C) wet and sad   (D) red and arid   (E) dry and hot

38. Which best describes Mr. Beech's attitude when he said "'A beautiful monarch, truly, with your two leaves and not a sign of a crown!'"?

(A) judgy   (B) benevolent   (C) humble   (D) considerate   (E) hopeful

39. Which word is synonymous to "ridicule"?

(A) praise   (B) mockery   (C) commendation   (D) reward   (E) esteem

40. Which best concludes the moral of the story?

(A) mockery is everywhere anytime so stay proud

(B) Do not let other people dim your light. Work hard in silence and let your triumph make the noise

(C) honesty is the best policy

(D) there is no better advice than criticism

(E) be the first to judge

SECTION 4

VERBAL REASONING

Time—30 minutes
60 Questions

Directions: This section is divided into two parts that contain different types of questions. As soon as you have completed part one, answer the questions in part two. You may write in your test booklet. For each answer you select, fill in the corresponding circle on your answer document.

PART ONE

Directions: Each question in part one is made up of a word in capital letters followed by five choices. Choose a word that is most nearly the same in meaning as the word in capital letters.

Example	Answer
SWIFT: (A) clean (B) fancy (C) fast (D) quiet (E) noisy	Ⓐ Ⓑ ● Ⓓ Ⓔ

1. COPIOUS

    (A) lacking (B) meager (C) needing (D) scarce (E) abundant

2. CORDIAL

    (A) friendly (B) cold (C) disagreeable (D) rude (E) aloof

3. CORROSION

    (A) growth (B) decay (C) improvement (D) development (E) construction

4. COUNTERFEIT

    (A) actual (B) authentic (C) imitation (D) factual (E) genuine

5. COWER

    (A) face (B) meet (C) come out (D) tremble (E) challenge

6. CREDIBLE

    (A) unreliable (B) deceptive (C) dishonest (D) implausible (E) trustworthy

7. CUNNING

(A) smart (B) blunt (C) coarse (D) dull (E) ignorant

8. DEFIANT

(A) obedient (B) bold (C) respectful (D) submissive (E) subordinating

9. DEFICIENT

(A) abundant (B) perfect (C) faulty (D) adequate (E) strong

10. DEFT

(A) awkward (B) clumsy (C) ignorant (D) clever (E) slow

11. DEJECTION

(A) sadness (B) cheer (C) happiness (D) joy (E) excitement

12. DELIBERATE

(A) to happen or occur by chance

(B) to take the risks of

(C) to happen by fate

(D) to weigh in the mind

(E) to be carefree

13. DEPICT

(A) to conceal from sight

(B) to represent by

(C) to obstruct the view of

(D) to cover up

(E) to keep secret

14. DESPAIR

(A) the feeling that what is wanted can be had

(B) a person or thing in which expectations are centered

(C) loss of hope

(D) to look forward with desire

(E) confident expectation of something

15. DESOLATE

   (A) highly pleased

   (B) characterized by or indicative of pleasure

   (C) favored by fortune

   (D) obsessed by or quick to use the item indicated

   (E) barren or laid waste

16. DETEST

   (A) to feel abhorrence or hate of

   (B) to have a profoundly tender, passionate affection for

   (C) to hold in esteem or honor

   (D) to show regard or consideration for

   (E) to refrain from intruding upon

17. DETRIMENTAL

   (A) favorably disposed

   (B) inclined to approve, help, or support

   (C) not hostile or at variance

   (D) causing damage

   (E) easy to use, operate, understand

18. DEVIATE

   (A) in a straight line

   (B) to turn aside, as from a route, way, course, etc.

   (C) not closed or barred at the time

   (D) set so as to permit passage through the opening

   (E) having the interior immediately accessible

19. DEVOTION

   (A) a feeling of strong dislike, ill will

   (B) a feeling of aversion

   (C) earnest attachment to a cause, person, etc.

   (D) an instinctive contrariety or opposition in feeling

   (E) habitual dislike

20. DISAVOW

(A) receive with approval or favor

(B) to agree or consent to

(C) to respond or answer affirmatively to

(D) to undertake the responsibility

(E) to disown

21. DISPEL

(A) collect   (B) dismiss   (C) accept   (D) gather   (E) allow

22. DISPARAGE

(A) admire   (B) approve   (C) commend   (D) belittle   (E) compliment

23. DISSECT

(A) combine   (B) connect   (C) cut   (D) join   (E) unite

24. DISTEND

(A) compress   (B) condense   (C) deflate   (D) swell   (E) decrease

25. DISTORT

(A) alter   (B) preserve   (C) ascend   (D) improve   (E) increase

26. DOCILE

(A) determined   (B) compliant   (C) headstrong   (D) obstinate   (E) stubborn

27. DRASTIC

(A) nice   (B) calm   (C) collected   (D) harsh   (E) easy

28. DREAD

(A) pleasant   (B) pleasing   (C) awful   (D) welcomed   (E) wonderful

29. DRENCH

(A) dehydrate   (B) parch   (C) dry   (D) soak   (E) enlarge

30. DUBIOUS

(A) doubtful   (B) reliable   (C) honest   (D) truthful   (E) open

PART TWO

Directions: Each question below is made up of a sentence with one or two blanks. One blank indicates that one word is missing. Two blanks indicate that two words are missing. Each sentence is followed by four choices. Select a word or pair of words that will best complete the meaning of the sentence as a whole.

Example   Answer

Ann carried the box carefully so that she would not _____ the pretty glasses.   ● Ⓑ Ⓒ Ⓓ

(A) break
(B) fix
(C) open
(D) stop

Example   Answer

When our boat first crashed into the rocks we were _____, but we soon felt   ● Ⓑ Ⓒ Ⓓ
_____ when we realized that nobody was hurt.

(A) afraid; relieved
(B) happy; confused
(C) sleepy; sad
(D) sorry; angry

---

31. He waited for this opportunity and was _____ to lead the play.

    (A) sad (B) disinterested (C) eager (D) bored

32. This five-star hotel will welcome you with _____ furnishings, exceptional service, and a memorable experience.

    (A) elegant (B) distasteful (C) outdated (D) poor

33. To _____ the legs, it is recommended to wear high waisted bottoms to give the illusion of looking taller.

    (A) shorten (B) elongate (C) cut (D) round

34. The class representative must be _____ since he will be tasked to read the graduation speech at the ceremony.

    (A) apathetic (B) eloquent (C) calm (D) dull

35. The research will _____ multiple theories related to the origin of species.

    (A) sit (B) stand (C) laugh (D) embody

36. No eating and chatting in the library were _____ during the early assembly after yesterday's incident.

    (A) spoken (B) thought (C) emphasized (D) taught

37. Despite coming from a poor background, her parents continue to support her _____.

    (A) endeavors (B) irresponsibility (C) insanity (D) folly

38. The unsolved disappearance of these young women remains an _____ to the community.

    (A) enigma (B) inspiration (C) motivation (D) goal

39. It was a surprise to the class that the role was _____ to a shy boy who never spoke a word since the beginning of the school year.

    (A) modified (B) entrusted (C) captured (D) played

40. They gazed with eyes full of _____ as an unexpected winner was announced.

    (A) cheer (B) courtesy (C) envy (D) dream

41. Bryan was the _____ of goodness which is the reason he was _____ as the class representative.

    (A) chalice: dismissed (B) sample: disqualified (C) epitome: canceled (D) epitome: chosen

42. This year's Science forum goal was to _____ rotavirus with the help of doctors through _____ research.

    (A) eradicate: painstaking (B) promote: thorough (C) develop: lousy (D) improve: simple

43. There are many _____ that affect the _____ behavior of the value of a nation's currency.

    (A) sources: steady (B) studies: dead (C) factors: erratic (D) factors: flatline

44. Shiela will never _____ the gossips about her best friend as she holds her in high _____.

    (A) stop; regard (B) pause: esteem (C) believe: esteem (D) think: disrespect

45. They got _____ to _____ the tyrant school principal after loitering while classes are ongoing.

    (A) hopeless: escape (B) lucky: evade (C) disappointed: lose (D) hopeful: meet

46. The renter has been _____ for three months straight, so the landlord sent an _____ notice effective immediately.

(A) noncompliant: eviction   (B) compliant: eviction   (C) diligent: eviction   (D) hopeless: welcome

47. She was _____ to stay home so as not to _____ her symptoms.

(A) reprimanded: cure   (B) commanded: heal   (C) allowed: mend   (D) advised: exacerbate

48. Due to this honorary_____, he has been _____ to a higher rank.

(A) award: exalted   (B) discipline: lowered   (C) violation: raised   (D) crime: promoted

49. These _____ in shipment are _____ regular customers.

(A) advances: disappointing   (B) promptness: saddening

(C) delays: exasperating   (D) delays: enlightening

50. The archeologists used the latest _____ in _____ the recent sites.

(A) machinery: preserving   (B) tools: excavating   (C) gadgets: burying   (D) equipment: hiding

51. Exile is to refugee as immigrant is to _____.

(A) resident   (B) foreigner   (C) Eastern   (D) native

52. Extend is to expand as abbreviate is to _____.

(A) lengthen   (B) long   (C) shorten   (D) symbol

53. Extol is to applaud as criticize is to _____.

(A) humiliate   (B) praise   (C) feedback   (D) celebrate

54. Extravagant is to excessive as careful is to _____.

(A) careless   (B) thoughtless   (C) reasonable   (D) rash

55. Feeble is to frail as competent is to _____.

(A) inefficient   (B) weak   (C) able   (D) unable

56. Feisty is to timid as courageous is to _____.

(A) daring   (B) fearless   (C) gusty   (D) fearful

57. Fickle is to constant as stable is to _____.

    (A) unreliable (B) balanced (C) clam (D) secure

58. Flourish is to shrink as wither is to _____.

    (A) expand (B) decay (C) dry (D) deflate

59. Fragile is to durable as firm is to _____.

    (A) rigid (B) flexible (C) stiff (D) sturdy

60. Frugal is to wasteful as generous is to _____.

    (A) benevolent (B) kind (C) greedy (D) charitable

SECTION 5

QUANTITATIVE MATH

Time—30 minutes

25 Questions

Directions: Each question is followed by five suggested answers. Read each question and then decide which one of the five suggested answers is best.

Find the row of spaces on your answer document that has the same number as the question. In this row, mark the space having the same letter as the answer you have chosen. You may write in your test booklet.

Example

5,413 – 4,827 =

(A) 586
(B) 596
(C) 696
(D) 1,586
(E) 1,686

The correct answer to this question is lettered A, so space A is marked.

Answer

● Ⓑ Ⓒ Ⓓ Ⓔ

---

1. How many factors does 36 have?

   (A) 9 (B) 5 (C) 12 (D) 7 (E) 3

2. Which of the following are complementary angles?

   (A) 90° and 90° (B) 45° and 90° (C) 60° and 120° (D) 50° and 40° (E) 100° and 80°

3. Find the area of the rectangle if the length is 11 ft and the width is 8.5 ft.

   (A) 94.5 ft² (B) 93.5 ft² (C) 39.5 ft² (D) 59.3 ft² (E) 95.3 ft²

4. Which number equals to 5^{-3}?

   (A) –125 (B) 125 (C) $-\dfrac{1}{125}$ (D) $\dfrac{1}{125}$ (E) –25

5. A circle has a circumference of 50 ft approximately, what is its diameter?

   (A) 11.51 ft (B) 12.5 ft (C) 11.42 ft (D) 12.73 ft (E) 15.9 ft

6. What is the fifth term of the following sequence? $1, \frac{3}{4}, \frac{1}{2}, \frac{1}{4},$ _____

   (A) $\frac{2}{4}$ (B) $\frac{1}{8}$ (C) $\frac{1}{3}$ (D) $\frac{2}{3}$ (E) 0

7. A circle on a coordinate plane has an equation of $x^2 + y^2 = 81$. What is the circumference of the circle?

   (A) 21π (B) 15π (C) 18π (D) 9π (E) 24π

8. Evaluate: $(11^4)^7$

   (A) 11^{28} (B) 11^{11} (C) 11 (D) 11^1 (E) 11^{15}

9. Evaluate: $-4(-9)^2$

   (A) 423 (B) 244 (C) 324 (D) 234 (E) 342

10. Combine and simplify: $(2x^5 - 7x^3 + 4) - (7x^5 - 3x^4 + x^2 + 8)$

    (A) $-5x^5 + 3x^4 - 7x^3 - x^2 - 4$ (B) $-5x^5 - 3x^4 - 7x^3 - x^2 + 12$ (C) $-5x^5 - 3x^4 - 7x^3 - x^2 - 4$

    (D) $5x^5 + 3x^4 - 7x^3 - x^2 + 4$ (E) $5x^5 - 3x^4 - 7x^3 - x^2 + 4$

11. Let b represents the base of a rectangle and h be the height. If the height of the rectangle is 4 less than the base, which expression would represent the perimeter of the rectangle?

    (A) $4b - 8$ (B) $2b - 4$ (C) $2b - 2$ (D) $2b + 4$ (E) $4b - 4$

12. What is the y-intercept of the graph of the function: $f(x) = 11x^2 + 4x + 8$

    (A) $(0, 4)$ (B) $(4, 0)$ (C) $(0, 8)$ (D) $(8, 0)$ (E) cannot be determined

13. Two perpendicular lines intersect at the origin; one line also passes through point $(2,9)$. What is the slope of the other line?

    (A) $\frac{9}{2}$ (B) $-\frac{9}{2}$ (C) $\frac{1}{3}$ (D) $-\frac{1}{3}$ (E) cannot be determined

14. If the vertex angle of an isosceles triangle is $58°$, what is the value of one of its base angles?

    (A) $55°$ (B) $61°$ (C) $42°$ (D) $68°$ (E) $51°$

15. A spherical balloon has a diameter of 5 m. Give the volume of the balloon.

    (A) 63.45 m^3 (B) 67.45 m^3 (C) 64.45 m^3 (D) 65.45 m^3 (E) 66.45 m^3

16. The first two terms of an arithmetic sequence are 5 and 12, in that order. Give the one-hundredth term of that sequence.

    (A) 705 (B) 712 (C) 684 (D) 691 (E) 698

17. What is the reciprocal of 0.16?

(A) 6.52 (B) 5.62 (C) 6.25 (D) 5.26 (E) 2.56

18. If Nick's school is 3.8 miles away from his house, how far is it in feet?

(A) 20,064 ft (B) 20,460 ft (C) 20,640 ft (D) 20,044 ft (E) 20,046 ft

19. The average of five consecutive even integers is 28. What is the greatest number of these integers?

(A) 36 (B) 34 (C) 28 (D) 26 (E) 32

20. If 8 + 10 + N = 7 + 9 + 11, then what is the value of N?

(A) 11 (B) 7 (C) 15 (D) 9 (E) 5

21. 3 × 16 × 5 × 2 is equal to the product of 30 and what number?

(A) 14 (B) 10 (C) 16 (D) 20 (E) 18

22. If $\frac{2}{3}$ of a number is 88, then what is $\frac{1}{4}$ of the same number?

(A) 24 (B) 33 (C) 20 (D) 40 (E) 39

23. Kayla bought a box of chocolates that has 20 pieces. If 12 pieces have almonds in them, what percent of the chocolates are without almonds?

(A) 30% (B) 40% (C) 60% (D) 35% (E) 50%

24. What is the decimal form of $9\frac{3}{4}\%$?

(A) 9.75 (B) 0.975 (C) 0.0975 (D) 0.00975 (E) 0.000975

25. If $14a + 4a - 8a = 92$, then what is the value of a?

(A) 9 (B) 8.4 (C) 9.2 (D) 8.8 (E) 9.6

Answer Key

Section 1

⟨ Topic: The impact of technology to our daily lives. ⟩

The human race is indeed a superior species, and we just keep on striving for more improvement. We have come extremely far from when humans first discovered fire. Inventions created both useful and terrifying creations.

For instance, technology is the greatest invention man has ever made. From simple kitchen appliances to man reaching the moon and exploring space. Can you imagine a day without your phone or internet? What will happen to the world if internet suddenly turns off?

In the recent health crisis, technology played an important role in ensuring daily lives continue despite the home arrest. We were able to continue working at the comforts of our homes and send children to school virtually. We were able to connect with people despite the distance while keeping everyone safe. We were able to live through the new normal with the help of technology.

If the health crisis had happened when advanced technology was not available yet, what could have happened? In addition to not being able to continue school and work, technology also had a vital role in fighting the virus. Technology made it possible to develop these tests, treatments, and vaccines at such a fast pace. Even long before the recent health crisis, technology, together with medicine, has played hand in hand in treating known diseases to mankind. It has significantly made lives more convenient.

There is no doubt that technology has been beneficial to us, but it also gave birth to the dangers one could have never imagined. For example, invention of mobile vehicles has made travels faster and easier but also made our air polluted. Carbon monoxide emitted by vehicles caused air pollution which poses danger not only to humans. Factories produce greenhouse gases that caused our destruction to the ozone layer making us vulnerable to the harmful rays of the sun. Easy access to mobile gadgets has become a problem to children's health. Don't get me started with radiation and access to destructive weaponries used in wars affecting the innocent.

Technology has been both boon and bane of our existence. It is up to us which side we want our future to become.

Section 2

1. D	6. A	11. E	16. C	21. D
2. A	7. E	12. C	17. A	22. B
3. C	8. B	13. D	18. A	23. D
4. C	9. D	14. E	19. C	24. A
5. B	10. A	15. B	20. B	25. C

1. **Answer: D**

   Let's get the measures of the length and width of the rectangle. $P = 2l + 2w \Rightarrow 160 = 2(3w) + 2w \Rightarrow 160 = 8w \Rightarrow w = 20, l = 60$. Now that we have the measures of the dimensions, solve for the area. $A = l \times w = 60 \times 20 = 1200$. The area of the rectangle is 1200 mm², hence the answer is D.

2. **Answer: A**

   To get the surface area of a cube, use the formula $SA = 6s^2 = 6(12.5)^2 = 6(156.25) = 937.5$. The surface area of the cube is 937.5 in², hence the answer is A.

3. **Answer: C**

   Let's first get the discount: $189 \times \dfrac{55}{100} = 103.95$. Now that we have the discount, let's then subtract it from the original price: $189 - 103.95 = 85.05$. The new cost of the shoes is $85.05, hence the answer is C.

4. **Answer: C**

   Add the allocated percentage for Mathilda's taxes and insurance: $15\% + 3\% = 18\%$. The total percentage taken out of Mathilda's paycheck is 18%, hence the answer is C.

5. **Answer: B**

   The sum of the external angles of any triangle, including an equilateral triangle, is always 360°, hence the answer is B.

6. **Answer: A**

   Divide the total number of planners and the number of planners that could fit in one box: $25 \div 5 = 5$. Andrew must buy 5 boxes of planners, hence the answer is A.

7. **Answer: E**

   Let's first multiply the 12 bouquets with Lucy's standard rate: $12 \times 14 = \$168$. For the additional bouquets, let's then multiply it with $17.50: $10 \times 17.50 = \$175$. Let's add: $\$168 + \$175 = \$343.00$. Lucy will receive $343.00, hence the answer is E.

8. **Answer: B**

   Let's get the sum of the length of the hamsters. For the four female hamsters, let's multiply 4 to the average length to get their sum: $5.7 \times 4 = 22.8$. Do the same for the male hamsters: $6.3 \times 7 = 44.1$. Let's then get the average of all the hamsters: $\dfrac{22.8 + 44.1}{11} = 6.08$ in. The average length of all hamsters is 6.08 in, hence the answer is B.

9. **Answer: D**

   To get the number of students uses smartphones and laptops, use the formula $G_1 + G_2 + N - B = T$ which means Group 1 + Group 2 + Neither − Both = Total. "Group 1" will be the students that uses smartphones, "Group 2" for those that uses laptop, "Neither" will be 0 since it did not mention that the students use other gadgets aside the two devices. Solve: $150 + 75 + 0 - B = 200 \Rightarrow 225 - B = 200 \Rightarrow B = 25$. The number of students that uses both smartphones and laptops is 25, hence the answer is D.

10. Answer: **A**

Let's multiply $80 with 24 months (2 years) and add the down payment: 80 × 12 = $1920 + $1000 = $2920. Subtract the result with the selling price: $2920 − $2250 = $670. Mr. Clint has to pay $670 more, hence the answer is A.

11. Answer: **E**

Let's get the average: $\left(\dfrac{15}{3} + 45.8\right) \div 2 = \dfrac{5 + 45.8}{2} = \dfrac{50.8}{2} = 25.4$. The average is 25.4, hence the answer is E.

12. Answer: **C**

Let x be the number: $5x + 72 = 247 \implies 5x = 175 \implies x = 35$. The number is 35, hence the answer is C.

13. Answer: **D**

Let's use elimination to get the answer. We can assume that $K + L = 160$, so K and L can be any integers that will have a sum of 160. Options A, B, and C cannot be true. Let's manipulate option D, by adding K and 80 and we will have $160 = L + K$ or $K + L = 160$, hence the answer is D.

14. Answer: **E**

Let x be the number of anime cards in Ken's collection. When he gave 40% of the card collection to Sabrina, he was left with 60% or $0.6x$. He then, gave 40% of the remaining cards, which is $(0.4)(0.6x)$ or $0.24x$. What was left is $0.6x - 0.24x = 0.36x$. Ken still has 36% of his anime card collection, hence the answer is E.

15. Answer: **B**

Let's multiply the original price of the ticket with the percentage Farrah is planning to sell it for: 58.94 × 0.57 = 33.60. Farrah will sell her ticket for $33.60, hence the answer is B.

16. Answer: **C**

To get the volume of a sphere, we use the formula $V = \dfrac{4}{3}\pi r^3 \implies 1000 = \dfrac{4}{3}\pi r^3 \implies r^3 = 238.85 \implies r = 6.2$ in. The diameter is twice the radius (r), so let's multiply the radius by 2: 6.2 × 2 = 12.4 in. The diameter is 12.4 in, hence the answer is C.

17. Answer: **A**

The formula to get the perimeter of a regular hexagon is $P = 6s$. We can use to get the length of each side. $P = 6s \implies 45 = 6s \implies s = 7.5$ ft. Each side measures 7.5 ft, hence the answer is A.

18. Answer: **A**

Let's get the total number of marbles: 7 blue + 9 red + 4 yellow = 20 marbles. The probability of Ross getting a blue marble is $\dfrac{7}{20}$ or 35%, hence the answer is A.

19. **Answer: C**

    Let x be the smallest number, $x + 2$ be the second largest number and $x + 4$ be the largest number.

    $x + x + 4 = 152 \Rightarrow 2x = 148 \Rightarrow x = 74$. We have now the value of the smallest number. Substitute the value of x to get the second largest number: $x + 2 = 74 + 2 = 76$. The second largest number is 76, hence the answer is C.

20. **Answer: B**

    Let's first get the slope of the line $2x + 4y = 8$: $4y = -2x + 8 \Rightarrow y = -\frac{1}{2}x + 2$. The slope of this line $-\frac{1}{2}$. A perpendicular line's slope would be the negative reciprocal of that value, which is 2, hence the answer is B.

21. **Answer: D**

    To find the percentage for year 2020, add the changes each year to the initial percentage: $29\% + 3\% + (-1\%) + (-1\%) + 4\% + 7\% = 41\%$. The cosmetics sold for 2020 was 41%, hence the answer is D.

22. **Answer: B**

    To get the amount of Marissa's parents' contribution, we can use the formula $\left(\frac{s_1 + s_n}{2}\right) \cdot n$, where S_1 is the first amount, S_n is the last amount and n is the total number of miles. As you can observe, every mile, there will be an additional \$2.00. If Marissa will run 18 miles, then her parents will donate \$36 on the 18th mile. Let's solve: $\left(\frac{2 + 36}{2}\right) \cdot 18 = 19 \times 18 = 342$. Marissa's parents' total contribution will be \$342.00, hence the answer is B.

23. **Answer: D**

    Let's first get perimeter of the square. $P = 4s = 4(12) = 48$ cm. Since the perimeter of the equilateral triangle is half of the perimeter of the square, then the perimeter of the triangle is 24 cm. To get the length of side of the triangle, use the formula $P = 3s$: $24 = 3s \Rightarrow s = 8$ cm. A side of the equilateral triangle is 8 cm, hence the answer is D.

24. **Answer: A**

    Each flip of the coin is an independent event, so the previous nine results won't affect the 10th flip. What matters is that the coin is fair. Since there's only two faces of a coin, heads and tails, then the probability that the coin will be heads is one out of two results or $\frac{1}{2}$, hence the answer is A.

25. **Answer: C**

    Let's get the area of the farm: $A = l \times w = 350 \times 150 = 52{,}000$ sq ft. Let's divide the area by 60 sq ft to get the total pounds of fertilizer needed. $52{,}000 \div 60 = 875$. Next, let's multiply it to the cost of each pound: $875 \times 3.70 = \$3{,}237.50$. Mr. Rivera needs to spend \$3,237.50 to fertilize his farm, hence the answer is C.

Section 3

1.	C	6.	D	11.	B	16.	C	21.	D	26.	B	31.	C	36.	E
2.	A	7.	A	12.	C	17.	A	22.	A	27.	C	32.	C	37.	A
3.	B	8.	C	13.	A	18.	B	23.	C	28.	A	33.	B	38.	D
4.	B	9.	C	14.	C	19.	B	24.	C	29.	C	34.	A	39.	B
5.	D	10.	E	15.	C	20.	D	25.	B	30.	C	35.	D	40.	B

1. The correct answer is C. The passage introduced Hawaii being the only state that currently has amended the constitution to include the right to a healthy environment. This has been the basis in rejecting the proposal of a biomass plant to burn eucalyptus trees and other invasive species in exchange of planting 3.1 million trees to offset its carbon emissions.

2. The correct answer is A. Hawaii is the first in the nation to declare a climate emergency in 2021, asserting that the right to a healthy environment is a basic human right, as proclaimed decades earlier in the state constitution. Honolulu is a city in Hawaii.

3. The correct answer is B. Hawaii is the first in the nation to declare a climate emergency in 2021, asserting that the right to a healthy environment is a basic human right, as proclaimed decades earlier in the state constitution. Honolulu is a city in Hawaii.

4. The correct answer is B. Hawaii is in a climate emergency and the state bears a constitutional duty to limit greenhouse gas emissions to prevent additional global warming. Climate change is "a human rights issue at its core," and it disproportionately harms youth, future generations, and Native peoples.

5. The correct answer is D. This news sheds a better light that it is possible for a state to make healthy environment a right and take charge in fighting climate change.

6. The correct answer is D. To assert means to state with assurance, confidence, or force; state strongly or positively; affirm; aver.

7. The correct answer is A. The passage gives us information on how Hawaii decides on state decisions that may worsen climate change in accordance with the state's constitutional duty to limit greenhouse gas emissions to prevent additional global warming.

8. The correct answer is C. The passage was about gap year and the programs and options available for those who undergo it. It talks about the objectives of gap year and how it can help high school graduates choose better paths before they proceed to college.

9.   The correct answer is C. A gap year is described as a natural break to delay college where high school graduates choose between electing to work to make money for college or earn internship credits or explore to help them make better choices before they go to college.

10. The correct answer is E. Students may also elect to work during a gap year, either to make money for college or to earn college credit through an internship. "The best gap years tend to be the ones that push students to think about who they are and their role in the world," says Joe O'Shea. She says a gap year can help motivate and inspire students and better prepare them for college.

11. The correct answer is B. For high school students or graduates considering a gap year, the options are plentiful and include structured programs or self-guided exploration.

12. The correct answer is C. The Gap Year Association, which accredits numerous programs, lists experiences with a focus on ecology, animal welfare, and conservation, language studies, coding, cultural immersion, and a variety of other topics.

13. The correct answer is A. To accredit means to certify (a school, college, or the like) as meeting all formal official requirements of academic excellence, curriculum, facilities, etc.

14. The correct answer is C. The passage was a news article about a dangerously overcrowded ship that drifted the Italian waters before getting rescued after days being afloat Mediterranean.

15. The correct answer is C. According to the news, "Written communication received by the AFM from the ship captain providing duty of care confirms that no rescue was requested by the people on board." It was not clear which ship captain the statement was referring to, and representatives from Malta did not respond to several requests for follow-up comment. Malta's, FMT URLA's and Pericles' responses fell far short of what was required of them.

16. The correct answer is C. Eventually, on April 12, when the ship drifted into Italian waters, that country's coast guard dispatched rescue vessels and brought the starving migrants to their shores.

17. The correct answer is A. Purportedly means according to what is or has been claimed, reputed, or asserted; allegedly.

18. The correct answer is B. Suspenseful means hair-raising or a feeling usually accompanied by a degree of apprehension or anxiety. Not being rescued for days suffering from cold temperatures, hunger, and thirst is not a joyful experience.

19. The correct answer is B. Purportedly means according to what is or has been claimed, reputed, or asserted; allegedly.

20. The correct answer is D. The article mainly talks about how extra attention and worry over what is causing your flu symptoms are not necessary unless you have a weak immune system.

21. The correct answer is D. Extra attention, worry over what is causing your flu symptoms, and over-testing are not necessary unless you have a weakened immune system.

22. The correct answer is A. For healthy people with mild cold symptoms, doctors say these tests are not worth the cost because treatment—hydration, rest, cough suppressants if needed—is the same for most viruses since viral infections are not treatable with antibiotics.

23. The correct answer is C. For healthy people with mild cold symptoms, doctors say these tests are not worth the cost because treatment—hydration, rest, cough suppressants if needed—is the same for most viruses since viral infections are not treatable with antibiotics.

24. The correct answer is C. A surge means a sudden, strong increase or burst.

25. The correct answer is B. The passage is from the story "A Horse's Tale" which is narrated by Buffalo Bill's horse. The horse talks about how he sees himself as part of Buffalo Bill's magnificent appearance as he described himself saying "he is a sight to look at then—and I'm part of it myself."

26. The correct answer is B. The passage is from the story "A Horse's Tale" which is narrated by Buffalo Bill's horse. The horse talks about how he sees himself as part of Buffalo Bill's magnificent appearance as he described himself saying "he is a sight to look at then—and I'm part of it myself."

27. The correct answer is C. The passage is from the story "A Horse's Tale" which is narrated by Buffalo Bill's horse.

28. The correct answer is A. As narrated by this sentence "Big as he is, I have carried him eighty-one miles between nightfall and sunrise on the scout" and as described by the narrator, Buffalo Bill is possibly a scout or someone from the police.

29. The correct answer is C. Springy means characterized by spring or elasticity; flexible; resilient.

30. The correct answer is C. An express may be a train or a bus. In the passage, the second sentence states that the loungers are at the Summerville station which indicates they are at a train station.

31. The correct answer is C. It was described as a hot day, sultry night; therefore, it was probably in summer.

32. The correct answer is C. It was described as a hot day, sultry night; therefore, it was probably in summer. Sweltering means suffering oppressive heat.

33. The correct answer is B. An excursionist is a person who goes on an excursion; a tourist or a traveler.

34. The correct answer is A. In the passage, it was said that the ice-cream placards of the merchant were well rewarded that scorching night. Therefore, his business hit off because of the favorable weather to have an ice-cream.

35. The correct answer is D. The passage was about Aunt Eunice telling her nieces a fairy story about a little Oak and his encounter with the fairy.

36. The correct answer is E. In the passage, as Aunt Eunice was about to start her story, both girls asked in a breath if she was telling them a fairy story, which implied they were anticipating.

37. The correct answer is A. In the story, the forest was string to bloom again after a dark winter which signifies the start of spring. Spring is also called the budding or flowering season.

38. The correct answer is D. Mr. Beech said the statement in disdain as he criticized the little Oak. Judgy is informal for tending to judge or criticize too quickly and harshly; judgmental.

39. The correct answer is B. Ridicule means speech or action intended to cause contemptuous laughter at a person or thing; derision.

40. The correct answer is B. The fairy went to the Oak after hearing the mockery from the other trees and uplifted his spirit. She told him to ignore them and keep on working with the sun and dew because soon he will be far above all of them both in position and fame.

Section 4

1. E	11. A	21. B	31. C	41. D	51. B
2. A	12. D	22. D	32. A	42. A	52. C
3. B	13. B	23. C	33. B	43. C	53. A
4. C	14. C	24. D	34. B	44. C	54. C
5. D	15. E	25. A	35. D	45. B	55. C
6. E	16. A	26. B	36. C	46. A	56. D
7. A	17. D	27. D	37. A	47. D	57. A
8. B	18. B	28. C	38. A	48. A	58. A
9. C	19. C	29. D	39. B	49. C	59. B
10. D	20. E	30. A	40. C	50. B	60. C

1. The correct answer is E. Copious means large in quantity or number; abundant; plentiful.

2. The correct answer is A. Cordial means courteous and gracious; friendly; warm.

3. The correct answer is B. Corrosion means the act or process of corroding; condition of being corroded. To corrode means to impair; deteriorate.

4. The correct answer is C. Counterfeit means made in imitation so as to be passed off fraudulently or deceptively as genuine; not genuine; forged.

5. The correct answer is D. To cower means to crouch, as in fear or shame.

6. The correct answer is E. Credible means worthy of belief or confidence; trustworthy.

7. The correct answer is A. Cunning means showing or made with ingenuity; skillful; expert.

8. The correct answer is B. Defiant means characterized by defiance; boldly resistant or challenging.

9. The correct answer is C. Deficient means lacking some element or characteristic; defective.

10. The correct answer is D. Deft means dexterous; nimble; skillful; clever.

11. The correct answer is A. Dejection is depression or lowness of spirits.

12. The correct answer is D. To deliberate means to weigh in the mind; to consider.

13. The correct answer is B. To depict means to represent by or as if by painting or other visual image; portray; delineate.

14. The correct answer is C. Despair means loss of hope; hopelessness.

15. The correct answer is E. Desolate means barren or laid waste; devastated.

16. The correct answer is A. To detest means to feel abhorrence of; hate; dislike intensely.

17. The correct answer is D. Detrimental means causing detriment, as loss or injury; damaging; harmful.

18. The correct answer is B. To deviate means to turn aside, as from a route, way, course, etc.

19. The correct answer is C. Devotion means earnest attachment to a cause, person, etc.

20. The correct answer is E. To disavow means to disclaim knowledge of, connection with, or responsibility for; disown; repudiate.

21. The correct answer is B. To dispel means to drive off in various directions; disperse; dissipate.

22. The correct answer is D. To disparage means to bring reproach or discredit upon; lower the estimation of.

23. The correct answer is C. To dissect means to cut apart (an animal body, plant, etc.) to examine the structure, relation of parts, or the like.

24. The correct answer is D. To distend means to expand by stretching, as something hollow or elastic.

25. The correct answer is A. To distort means to twist awry or out of shape; make crooked or deformed.

26. The correct answer is B. Docile means easily managed or handled; tractable.

27. The correct answer is D. Drastic means extremely severe or extensive.

28. The correct answer is C. Dread means greatly feared; frightful; terrible.

29. The correct answer is D. To drench means to get wet thoroughly; soak.

30. The correct answer is A. Dubious means doubtful; marked by or occasioning doubt.

31. The correct answer is C. Eager means keen or ardent in desire or feeling; impatiently longing.

32. The correct answer is A. Elegant means tastefully fine or luxurious in dress, style, design, etc.

33. The correct answer is B. To elongate means to draw out to greater length; lengthen; extend.

34. The correct answer is B. Eloquent is having or exercising the power of fluent, forceful, and appropriate speech.

35. The correct answer is D. To embody means to collect into or include in a body; organize; incorporate.

36. The correct answer is C. To emphasize means to give emphasis to; lay stress upon; stress.

37. The correct answer is A. Endeavor means a strenuous effort; attempt.

38. The correct answer is A. Enigma means a puzzling or inexplicable occurrence or situation.

39. The correct answer is B. To entrust means to commit (something) in trust to; confide, as for care, use, or performance.

40. The correct answer is C. Envy is a feeling of discontent or covetousness with regard to another's advantages, success, possessions, etc.

41. The correct answer is D. Epitome means a person or thing that is typical of or possesses to a high degree the features of a whole class.

42. The correct answer is A. To eradicate means to remove or destroy utterly; extirpate. Painstaking means taking or characterized by taking pains or trouble; expending or showing diligent care and effort; careful.

43. The correct answer is C. Erratic means inconsistent, irregular, or unpredictable.

44. The correct answer is C. Esteem means favorable opinion or judgment; respect or regard.

45. The correct answer is B. To evade means to elude or get away from someone or something by craft or slyness; escape.

46. The correct answer is A. To evict means to expel (a person, especially a tenant) from land, a building, etc., by legal process, as for nonpayment of rent. Noncompliant means failure or refusal to comply, as with a law, regulation, or term of a contract.

47. The correct answer is D. To exacerbate means to increase the severity, bitterness, or violence of (disease, ill feeling, etc.); aggravate.

48. The correct answer is A. To exalt means to raise in rank, honor, power, character, quality, etc.; elevate.

49. The correct answer is C. Exasperating means to irritate or provoke to a high degree; annoy extremely.

50. The correct answer is B. To excavate means to make hollow by removing the inner part; make a hole or cavity in; form into a hollow, as by digging.

51. The correct answer is B. The first word pair are synonyms. An exile is a refugee, or a person deported from a place. An immigrant is person from a foreign land or a foreigner.

52. The correct answer is C. The first word pair are synonyms. To extend means to make larger, longer, or expand. To abbreviate means to shorten or compress.

53. The correct answer is A. The first word pair are synonyms. To extol means to applaud or sing the praises of. To criticize means to humiliate or disapprove, judge as bad.

54. The correct answer is C. The first word pair are synonyms. Extravagant means excessive or indulgent, wasteful. Careful means reasonable or cautious; painstaking.

55. The correct answer is C. The first word pair are synonyms. Feeble means frail or not strong; ineffective. Competent means able or capable.

56. The correct answer is D. The first word pair are antonyms. Feisty is spirited which is the opposite of timid. Courageous is brave which is the opposite of fearful.

57. The correct answer is A. The first word pair are antonyms. Fickle means likely to change, especially due to caprice, irresolution, or instability; casually changeable which is the opposite of constant. Steady is fixed; resistant which is the opposite of unreliable.

58. The correct answer is A. The first word pair are antonyms. To flourish means to grow or prosper which is the opposite of to shrink. To wither means to decline which is the opposite of to expand.

59. The correct answer is B. The first word pair are antonyms. Fragile means feeble or delicate which is the opposite of durable. Firm is stable and unmoving which is the opposite of flexible.

60. The correct answer is C. The first word pair are antonyms. Frugal means economical which is the opposite of wasteful. Generous means charitable which is the opposite of greedy.

Section 5

1. A	6. E	11. A	16. E	21. C
2. D	7. C	12. C	17. C	22. B
3. B	8. A	13. B	18. A	23. B
4. D	9. C	14. B	19. E	24. C
5. E	10. A	15. D	20. D	25. C

1. Answer: **A**

    The factors of 36 are (1,36), (2,18), (3,12), (4,9), and (6,6). There's a total of 9 factors for 36, hence the answer is A.

2. Answer: **D**

    Complementary angles are two angles that add to 90°. Among the choices, only option D has the sum of 90° if you add the two angles, hence the answer is D.

3. Answer: **B**

    To get the area of a rectangle, use the formula $A = l \times w = 11 \times 8.5 = 93.5$ ft². The area of the rectangle is 93.5 ft², hence the answer is B.

4. Answer: **D**

    Solving for integers with negative exponent, use the rule $a^n = \dfrac{1}{a^n}$. $5^{-3} = \dfrac{1}{5^3} = \dfrac{1}{125}$. The answer is D.

5. Answer: **E**

To get the circumference of a circle, we can use the formula $C = \pi d$, where d is the diameter. Substitute and solve for d: $50 = \pi d \Rightarrow d = 15.9$. The diameter is approximately 15.9 ft, hence the answer is E.

6. Answer: **E**

The difference from first number to the next number is $\frac{1}{4}$. If we subtract $\frac{1}{4}$ from the fourth number, then the result will be 0. The fifth term is 0, hence the answer is E.

7. Answer: **C**

The equation of a circle on a coordinate plane is $x^2 + y^2 = r^2$, where r is the radius. In the equation $x^2 + y^2 = 81$, the radius will be 9, since the square root of 81 is 9. To get the circumference, we can use the formula $C = 2\pi r = 2\pi (9) = 18\pi$. The circumference is 18π, hence the answer is C.

8. Answer: **A**

A power raised to a power indicated that we multiply the two powers: $(a^n)^m = a^{nm}$. $(11^4)^7 = 11^{28}$. The answer is A.

9. Answer: **C**

Follow the PEMDAS rule. Let's solve number with exponent then multiply: $-4(-9)^2 = -4(81) = 324$. Answer is C.

10. Answer: **A**

Let's distribute -1 to the expression $(7x^5 - 3x^4 + x^2 + 8)$: $-7x^5 + 3x^4 - x^2 - 8$, then combine: $(2x^5 - 7x^3 + 4) + (-7x^5 + 3x^4 - x^2 - 8) = -5x^5 + 3x^4 - 7x^3 - x^2 - 4$. The answer is A.

11. Answer: **A**

The perimeter of a rectangle is $P = 2l + 2w$, but with the given dimensions, will be using base (b) and height (h) instead of length (l) and width (w). $P = 2b + 2h = 2b + 2(b - 4) = 2b + 2b - 8 = 4b - 8$. The perimeter of the rectangle would be $4b - 8$, hence the answer is A.

12. Answer: **C**

The y-intercept of a graph of a function is the point which it intersects the y-axis—that is with $x = 0$. The given will be $f(0) = 11x^2 + 4x + 8 = 11(0^2) + 4(0) + 8 = 8$. The y-intercept is $(0, 8)$, hence the answer is C.

13. Answer: **B**

Let's get the slope of the first line. Substitute $x_1 = 2$, $y_1 = 9$, $x_2 = 0$, $y_2 = 0$ in the slope formula: $m = \frac{y_1 - y_2}{x_1 - x_2} = \frac{9 - 0}{2 - 0} = \frac{9}{2}$. The slope of the first line is $\frac{9}{2}$. The slope of the perpendicular line will be the negative reciprocal of the first line which is $-\frac{2}{9}$, hence the answer is B.

14. Answer: **B**

In an isosceles triangle, the base angles are the same and all three angles of a triangle add up to 180°. Let's subtract the value of the vertex angle from 180°: 180 – 58 = 122. Let's divide the difference by two to get the value of each angle of the base: 122 ÷ 2 = 61. The value of one of the bases is 61°, hence the answer is B.

15. Answer: **D**

To get the volume of a sphere, we use the formula $V = \frac{4}{3}\pi r^3$. To get the radius, just divide the diameter to two which will be 2.5. Solve: $V = \frac{4}{3}\pi r^3 = \frac{4}{3}\pi(2.5)^3 = \frac{4}{3}\pi r^3 \approx 65.45$ m³. The volume is 65.45 m³, hence the answer is D.

16. Answer: **E**

The difference of the first number and the next number is 7, so we can assume that the common difference will 7 in this sequence to get the 100th term, let's use the formula: $x_{n-1} = x_0 + d(n - 1)$, where d is the common difference, n is the last term and x_0 is the first term. $x_{n-1} = x_0 + d(n - 1) \Rightarrow x_{99} = 1 + 5(100 - 1) = 5 + 7(99) = 698$. The 100th term is 698, hence the answer is E.

17. Answer: **C**

The reciprocal of a number is the quotient of 1 and that number. 1 ÷ 0.16 = 6.25. The reciprocal of 0.16 is 6.25, hence the answer is C.

18. Answer: **A**

In one mile, there's 5280 ft. Let's multiply: 3.8 × 5280 = 20,064. Nick's school is 20,064 ft away from his house, hence the answer is A.

19. Answer: **E**

The average of evenly-spaced number is also the median of those numbers, so the middle integer (3rd number) is also 28. The 4th number will be 30 and the 5th number will be 32. The greatest integer is 32, hence the answer is E.

20. Answer: **D**

Solve for N: 8 + 10 + N = 7 + 9 + 11 ⟹ 18 + N = 27 ⟹ N = 9. The value of N is 9, hence the answer is D.

21. Answer: **C**

Let x be the number: 3 × 16 × 5 × 2 = 30x ⟹ 480 = 30x ⟹ x = 16. The number is 16, hence the answer is C.

22. Answer: **B**

Let x be the number: $\frac{2}{3}x = 88 \Rightarrow x = 132$. The number is 132. Let's divide the number by four to get the $\frac{1}{4}$ of it: 132 ÷ 4 = 33. The answer is B.

23. Answer: **B**

Let's first get the percentage that has almonds: $\frac{12}{20} = 0.60 \times 100 = 60\%$. 60% of the chocolate have almonds. Let's subtract next to get the percentage of the chocolate without almonds: $100 - 60 = 40$. 40% of the chocolate are without almonds, hence the answer is B.

24. Answer: **C**

Let's convert the given to improper function $\frac{39}{4}\%$. Let's then divide it by 100 to get the decimal form: $\frac{39}{4} \div 100 = 0.0975$. The answer is C.

25. Answer: **C**

Solve for a: $14a + 4a - 8a = 92 \Rightarrow 10a = 92 \Rightarrow a = 9.2$. The value of a is 9.2, hence the answer is C.

SSAT Upper Level Exam 3

The
SSAT
+ Upper

SECTION 1

WRITING SAMPLE

Time—25 minutes

Directions: Using two sheets of lined theme paper, plan and write an essay on the topic assigned below. DO NOT WRITE ON ANOTHER TOPIC. AN ESSAY ON ANOTHER TOPIC IS NOT ACCEPTABLE.

Topic: The value of education to one's success.

Directions: How does the value of education affect one's success? Use reasons and specific examples to support your answer.

SECTION 2

QUANTITATIVE MATH

Time—35 minutes

25 Questions

Directions: Any figures that accompany questions in this section may be assumed to be drawn as accurately as possible EXCEPT when it is stated that a particular figure is not drawn to scale. Letter such as x, y, and n stand for real numbers.

Each question consists of a word problem followed by five answer choices. You may write in your text booklet; however, you may also be able to solve many of these problems in your head. Next, take a look at the five answer choices and select the best one.

Example

5,413 – 4,827 =

(A) 586
(B) 596
(C) 696
(D) 1,586
(E) 1,686

The correct answer to this question is lettered A, so space A is marked.

Answer

● Ⓑ Ⓒ Ⓓ Ⓔ

---

1. Leo plans to give a box of chocolates to each of her 55 party guests. There are 7 boxes of chocolates in each package. How many packages must he buy?

   (A) 11   (B) 5   (C) 8   (D) 7   (E) 10

2. A car company requires 104 lb of mass to engage the sensor for a passenger-side airbag. What is the smallest mass a person carrying a 4.5 kg backpack can be to ensure the sensor is engaged? (1 kg = 2.20 lbs.).

   (A) 94.1 lb   (B) 91.4 lb   (C) 41.9 lb   (D) 49.1 lb   (E) 104 lb

3. When 4,053 is divided by 82, the result is closest to which one of the following?

   (A) 49.501   (B) 49.327   (C) 44.927   (D) 49.601   (E) 49.427

4. What is the value of the greatest of four consecutive integers if the greatest number is 31 more than one-third of the least?

   (A) 42   (B) 46   (C) 45   (D) 43   (E) 44

5. The perimeter of a hexagon is 102 units. If the length of each side is reduced by 2 units, what is the perimeter of the new figure?

    (A) 100 units   (B) 95 units   (C) 102 units   (D) 90 units   (E) 97 units

6. Kim and Luis work on the same coffee shop downtown. Kim's house is 10 km away from the coffee shop and Luis's house is 12.5 km away. How far, in meters, is Kim's house from Luis's house?

    (A) 10 km   (B) 11.75 km   (C) 9.4 km   (D) 12.5 km   (E) cannot be determined

7. If 30% of a number is 222, what is 80% of that number?

    (A) 592   (B) 925   (C) 259   (D) 295   (E) 952

8. If m is a positive number and $n = \dfrac{1}{m}$, as m increases in value, what happens to n?

    (A) n increases   (B) n decreases   (C) n is unchanged

    (D) n increases then decreases   (E) cannot be determined

9. A train left from Regalia for Garden of Hesperides with the distance 300 miles. The train left at 9:40 a.m. and was scheduled to reach Garden of Hesperides at 3:30 p.m. If the train is travelling at 50 mph, will it arrive on or ahead of the scheduled time?

    (A) yes, it will arrive 10 minutes ahead of time   (B) yes, it will arrive 20 minutes early

    (C) yes, it will arrive exactly at the scheduled time   (D) no, it will be late by 5 minutes

    (E) no, it will be late by 10 minutes

10. A real estate investor buys a house and lot for $38,500. She pays $1625 to have it painted, $1975 to fix the plumbing, and $1400 for grading a driveway. At what price must she sell the property in order to make at least 15% profit?

    (A) $50,025   (B) $50,205   (C) $50,250   (D) $50,502   (E) $50,520

11. If $a = 4$, $b = 1$, $c = 7$, and $d = 2$, what is the value of $\sqrt{d(c+b) - a(b+d)}$?

    (A) 3   (B) 0   (C) 6   (D) 2   (E) 4

12. If a cheerleading team has 15 girls and 10 boys, approximately what percent of the team are girls?

    (A) 50%   (B) 75%   (C) 40%   (D) 60%   (E) 68%

13. Del has $560 in the bank. He took out 20% of it for a party expense. How much money will be left in his bank account?

    (A) $440   (B) $484   (C) $448   (D) $404   (E) $488

14. 42 is what percent of 120?

(A) 40%   (B) 35%   (C) 27%   (D) 52%   (E) 45%

15. Which number represents eight thousand three and seven thousandths?

(A) 8003.7   (B) 8003.07   (C) 8003.007   (D) 8003.0007   (E) 8003.00007

16. Madeline's golf balls each weighs 0.05 kilograms. She has 12 golf balls in a bag that weighs (including the bag) 0.84 kilograms. How many kilograms does the bag weigh by itself?

(A) 0.24 kg   (B) 0.42 kg   (C) 0.23 kg   (D) 0.32 kg   (E) 0.45 kg

17. Heidi purchased 5 peppers, 3 garlic, 9 onions, 2 carrots, and 1 pumpkin. What was the ratio of onions to all the items purchased?

(A) 4:5   (B) 1:4   (C) 1:5   (D) 3:20   (E) 9:20

18. The basketball team lost 18 games out of 27 games played. Find the ratio of the games won to the games lost.

(A) 1:2   (B) 2:1   (C) 4:8   (D) 8:4   (E) 18:9

19. If $k + 3 > 19$, then what would be the possible value of k?

(A) greater than 16   (B) less than 14   (C) less than 0   (D) equals to 10   (E) greater than 12

20. The shadow of a man 6 ft tall is 12 ft long. How tall is a tree that casts a 50 ft shadow? (Assuming that the shadows they cast are on the same direction).

(A) 20 ft   (B) 25 ft   (C) 15 ft   (D) 17 ft   (E) 22 ft

21. Four games drew an average of 29,500 people per game. If the attendance at the first three games was 22,600, 27,500, and 35,100, how many people attended the fourth game?

(A) 32,008   (B) 32,080   (C) 38,200   (D) 32,800   (E) 38,020

22. In three days, a point on the earth's surface rotates through an approximately what angle?

(A) 360°   (B) 720°   (C) 1,080°   (D) 540°   (E) 702°

23. A rectangle has a length of 15 m and a width of 9 m. What would be its area?

(A) 135 m²   (B) 153 m²   (C) 142 m²   (D) 124 m²   (E) 110 m²

24. One side of a square measure 7 in. How long will be the distance of the diagonal from one corner to the other?

    (A) $5\sqrt{2}$ in (B) $2\sqrt{7}$ in (C) $\sqrt{49}$ in (D) $2\sqrt{5}$ in (E) $7\sqrt{2}$ in

25. A plumber needs eight sections of pipe, each measure 22 cm long. If pipe is sold only by 70 cm per section, how many sections must he buy?

    (A) 1 (B) 3 (C) 5 (D) 2 (E) 4

READING COMPREHENSION

Time—40 minutes
40 Questions

Directions: This section contains seven short reading passages. Each passage is followed by several questions based on its content. Answer the questions following the passage on the basis of what is stated or implied in that passage. You may write in your test booklet.

Passage 1

The first speaker was a short, freckled-face boy, whose box strapped to his back identified him at once as a street boot-black. His hair was red, his fingers <u>defaced</u> by stains of blacking, and his clothing constructed on the most approved system of ventilation. He appeared to be twelve years old.

The boy whom he addressed as Ben was taller and looked older. He was probably not far from sixteen. His face and hands, though browned by exposure to wind and weather, were several shades cleaner than those of his companion. His face, too, was of a less common type. It was easy to see that, if he had been well dressed, he might readily have been taken for a gentleman's son. But in his present attire there was little chance of this mistake being made. His pants, marked by a green stripe, small around the waist and very broad at the hips, had evidently belonged to a Bowery swell; for the Bowery has its swells as well as Broadway, its more <u>aristocratic</u> neighbor. The vest had been discarded as a needless luxury; its place being partially supplied by a shirt of thick red flannel. This was by a frock-coat, which might once have belonged to a member of the Fat Men's Association, being aldermanic in its proportions. Now it was fallen from its high estate, its nap and original gloss had long departed, and it was <u>frayed</u> and torn in many places.

from Ben, the Luggage Boy by *Horatio Alger, Jr.*

1. The description of the two boys imply that they _____.

(A) are gentlemen's sons

(B) are scholars of a prestigious organization

(C) are of nobility

(D) belong to the lower-class society

(E) are enrolled to a boarding school

2. How is Ben distinguishable than the other boys?

   (A) he can easily be mistaken as a gentleman's son if dressed properly

   (B) he looked like an immigrant

   (C) his eye color is different than the rest

   (D) he speaks more languages than the other boys

   (E) he was the eldest

3. What does the word "aristocratic" mean?

   (A) of low grade or quality

   (B) violating generally accepted standards of good taste

   (C) having the manners, values, or qualities of a noble; elegant and stylish

   (D) unbecoming or unseemly

   (E) not in accordance with propriety of behavior, manners

4. Which among the words below is synonymous to the word "deface"?

   (A) build   (B) construct   (C) blemish   (D) repair   (E) adorn

5. Based on their description, we may assume that the boys are _____

   (A) fishermen   (B) ship crews   (C) students   (D) scholars   (E) laborers

6. What is the meaning of the word "frayed"?

   (A) neatly or tidily kept

   (B) worn to loose; raveled threads or fibers at the outer surface

   (C) having its original purity; uncorrupted or unsullied

   (D) free from spot or stain; spotlessly clean

   (E) free from fault or flaw; free from errors

7. Which is the most appropriate reaction after reading the passage?

   (A) jubilant that these boys have jobs to keep them off the streets

   (B) proud that they continue their education

   (C) pity for having to work hard at a young age instead of completing education

   (D) embarrassed that they wear such dirty clothes

   (E) irritated that they chose not to attend school

Passage 2

A train carrying <u>hazardous</u> materials derailed and a bridge collapsed into a southern Montana river Saturday, sending rail cars into the water and prompting concerns about contamination.

Some of those fears may have been <u>allayed</u> by evening as rail officials said two cars known to be carrying sodium hydro sulfate, which can burn, irritate and cause shortness of breath, had not entered the Yellowstone River below the failed bridge.

No hazardous materials were released from those particular rail cars, said Andy Garland, a spokesperson for Montana Rail Link.

But an unspecified number of other cars containing molten sulfur and asphalt had been "<u>compromised</u>," he said in a statement.

Officials will continue to monitor the derailment site, he said.

No injuries were reported, officials said.

As many as eight cars derailed, Columbus, Montana, Fire Chief Rich Cowger told NBC affiliate KULR of Billings.

Billings said in a statement that it would shut down city water system intakes fed by the Yellowstone River for the time any pollutant would need to pass and end up downstream.

Billings, a city of nearly 110,000 people, has a clean supply of drinking water in its system, including storage tanks that are full, it said.

from Train carrying hazardous materials derails and bridge collapses into Montana river by *Erick Mendoza and Dennis Romero, US News*

8. The passage is mainly about _____.

(A) the train incident carrying hazardous materials which could potentially contaminate the Yellowstone River

(B) the hazardous chemicals used in laboratory testing

(C) illegal transport of hazardous chemicals

(D) sickness due to the contaminated water

(E) shutting down the city water system due to contaminants from the helicopter crash

9. What is the main concern about the incident?

(A) potential cause of acid rain

(B) profit loss on the chemicals

(C) potential contamination of nearby water supplies

(D) people will try to retrieve the chemicals for personal profit

(E) important research may fail due to the incident

10. How did the officials respond to the incident?

(A) the officials were too busy, so they started investigating for contamination a week after the incident

(B) all officials went to the derailment site the morning after because the incident happened at night

(C) no contamination has been reported but officials will continue to monitor the derailment site and would shut down city water system if needed

(D) all water supplies were shut down leaving the nearby communities dependent to water sourced from other counties

(E) testing is ongoing after it was revealed that the water is contaminated

11. What does the word "compromised" mean?

(A) remaining uninjured, sound, or whole

(B) not changed or diminished

(C) containing all the elements properly belonging

(D) damaged, or flawed

(E) undivided; in one piece

12. What does the word "allayed" mean?

(A) put fear to rest

(B) made worse or more severe

(C) intensified, as anything evil

(D) caused to become irritated

(E) moved or force into violent

13. Which among the words is synonymous to "hazardous"?

(A) certain (B) definite (C) unsafe (D) secure (E) stable

Passage 3

They stopped to rest, and even the woman had a <u>weary</u>, jaded look.

"I feel as if I shall give up, some of these days." she exclaimed.

"O no mother!" the little girl answered, cheerfully. She was panting, with her hand on her side, and her face had a quiet, very sober look; only at those words a little pleasant smile broke over it.

"I shall," said the woman. "One can't stand everything, forever."

The little girl had not got over the panting yet, but standing there she struck up the sweet air and words.

"There is rest for the weary, There is rest for the weary, There is rest for the weary. There is rest for you."

"Yes, in the grave!" said the woman, bitterly. "There's no rest short for that, for mind or body."

"O yes, mother dear. For we which have believed do enter into rest. Jesus don't make us wait."

"I believe you eat the Bible and sleep on the Bible," said the woman, with a <u>faint</u> smile, taking at the same time a corner of her apron to wipe away a stray tear which had gathered in her eye. "I am glad it rests you, Nettie."

"And you, mother."

from Carpenter's daughter by *Susan Warner*

14. Which words best describe the little girl, Nettie?

   (A) unmotivated and tired

   (B) proud and arrogant

   (C) hopeful and optimistic

   (D) miserable and sad

   (E) anxious and weary

15. Which words best describe how the mother felt?

   (A) unmotivated and tired

   (B) proud and arrogant

   (C) hopeful and optimistic

   (D) miserable and sad

   (E) hopeless and pessimistic

16. What is the meaning of the word "weary"?

   (A) possessing or exhibiting energy

   (B) powerful in action or effect

   (C) physically or mentally exhausted

   (D) full or suggestive of life or vital energy

   (E) bustling with activity

17. Which sentence uses the word "jaded" correctly?

   (A) his angelic voice will warm even the jaded hearts

   (B) he jaded ran to train station

   (C) she jaded enthusiastically

   (D) regardless of jaded, nobody wins

   (E) I can't jaded him out

18. Which best describes the overall mood of the article?

    (A) overwhelmed in sorrow

    (B) filled with faith

    (C) deep and painful regret

    (D) full of contrition

    (E) apprehensive

19. Which among the words is synonymous to the word "faint"?

    (A) vivid (B) dull (C) bright (D) wide (E) sincere

Passage 4

Among the passengers that landed from the "Grace" were Mr. and Mrs. Halley. They were truly glad to let their eyes rest again upon their own old town and home. They had three children with them. Maurice had reached the mature age of ten; and a proud young gentleman he looked, as he stood by his father's side holding in his hand a beautiful cage of <u>considerable size</u>. The cage contained a fine young parrot which Maurice kept calling by all sorts of pet names, as often as he could withdraw his attention from his novel and exciting situation. Charles was only five years old as yet, and he pretended to no greater advancement in age. The poor little fellow was frightened at the roar and bustle on board and alarmed at the rush and crush on the quay, so he took refuge from them all by pressing as close as he could to his mother. Cecilia, only two years of age, was sound asleep in the arms of an elderly nurse, named Sally. Little sister Cissy recognized no difference between <u>sultry</u> India and sunny France. Sally's arms were the home and native land she loved with all the affection and patriotism she nursed as yet in her true heart. There was nothing in the all the bustle which drove Charles to his mother to disturb her comfortable sleep. Jacob, a faithful negro, was watchful and busy after the luggage.

from Lost Father by *Daryl Holme*

20. The passage implied that Mr. and Mrs. Halley's family _____.

    (A) are impoverished

    (B) is known in the field of medicine

    (C) is from a well-known clan

    (D) belongs to the middle to upper class

    (E) has multiple business ventures

21. "Pressing as close as he could to his mother" implies that, Charles _____.

    (A) is ignorant and mocks his mother

    (B) is lazy and depends on his mother

    (C) is brave and loves his mother

    (D) is frightened and feels most safe with his mother

    (E) is young and looks up to his mother

22. What does "considerable size" mean?

(A) rather large   (B) miniscule   (C) extra small   (D) unseen by the naked eye   (E) scarce

23. Which word is synonymous to "sultry"?

(A) cold   (B) freezing   (C) hot   (D) frigid   (E) chilled

24. How old is Mr. and Mrs. Halley's eldest child?

(A) 2 years old

(B) 5 years old

(C) 10 years old

(D) 10 years older than Charles

(E) 10 years older than Cecilia

Passage 5

A firefighter in Ocala, Florida, was pulling an overnight shift at the station in January when he was awakened at 2 a.m. by an alarm.

He recognized the sound immediately. A newborn had been placed in the building's Safe Haven Baby Box, a device that allows someone to safely and anonymously surrender a child—no questions asked.

"To be honest, I thought it was a false alarm," said the firefighter, who wished to remain anonymous to protect his family's privacy. But when he opened the box, he discovered a healthy infant wrapped in a pink blanket.

That baby would become his daughter, Zoey.

Zoey was placed in the station's Safe Haven Baby Box on Jan. 2. On Jan. 4, she was home with the firefighter and his wife. The couple adopted Zoey in April. The firefighter said he later learned from the hospital that the baby's umbilical cord had been tied off with a shoelace.

"The way I found her ... this was God helping us out," he said, adding that it's difficult not to cry when he tells the story.

He said he's sharing the story in that it gives Zoey's biological mother "some closure."

"We want her to know that her child is taken care of and that she's loved beyond words," he said.

from Newborn left in Florida Safe Haven Baby Box adopted by the firefighter who found her by *Rachel Abrahamson, TODAY*

25. What is the passage about?

(A) about a firefighter's job

(B) about a firefighter's answered prayer

(C) about a firefighter's struggle with infertility

(D) about abandoned babies

(E) about abortion

26. Which best describes the passage?

    (A) belittling and discouraging

    (B) touching and heartwarming

    (C) sad and lonely

    (D) depressing and nerve wracking

    (E) creepy and dangerous

27. What is the Safe Haven Baby Box?

    (A) an ovum and sperm cell donation box

    (B) a kit box where baby supplies are donated

    (C) a device that allows someone to surrender a child safely and anonymously

    (D) a device that allows someone to surrender a child and register their names

    (E) a kit box where baby supplies can be taken for free

28. Which word is synonymous to "anonymously"?

    (A) nameless   (B) known   (C) named   (D) identified   (E) distinguished

29. What does "loved beyond words" mean?

    (A) selfish love

    (B) unrequited love

    (C) overwhelming love

    (D) one-sided love

    (E) forbidden love

Passage 6

There is new evidence that measles cases are <u>ticking up</u> again in the U.S. after falling during lockdown.

As of June 8, "the United States has seen an increase in measles cases during the first 5 months of 2023, with 16 reported cases compared with 3 in 2022 during the same period," the CDC wrote in the health alert.

Eighty-eight percent of those cases have been linked to international travel. Most patients had not been vaccinated.

Just this week, health officials in California confirmed two measles cases from one household in Fresno County. There was no word on how the two people became infected.

"These cases are reminders of the critical role of vaccinations in protecting the community," Dr. Rais Vohra, Fresno County's health officer, said in a statement to NBC News. "We <u>urge</u> all parents to please work with your pediatrician or contact the health department to help get your child up-to-date on vaccinations."

In 2019, two large outbreaks in New York sent cases soaring to levels not seen since 1992: 1,274 cases.

New outbreaks are increasingly reported in other areas of the world, too, especially India, Indonesia, parts of the Middle East and much of Africa, the CDC said.

In the United Kingdom, health officials say that since the beginning of the year, there have been 49 cases of measles, compared to 54 cases during all of last year.

To best prevent measles outbreaks, 95% of a community should be vaccinated, according to the CDC. But vaccination rates declined during the pandemic, leading to pockets of vulnerability.

from A Lost Hero by Elizabeth Stuart Phelps

30. What is the objective of the passage?

   (A) encourage people to continue lockdown and house arrest

   (B) educate readers that there is no need to be vaccinated for measles during the pandemic

   (C) educate the people of the increasing measles cases and encourage vaccination

   (D) persuade readers that COVID 19 vaccination is all they need to avoid any virus

   (E) dissuade people from getting any more vaccinations

31. Where are the increasing measles cases in the United States attributed to?

   (A) due to back to school

   (B) this increase has been linked to opening public places to gather such as parks, clubs, etc.

   (C) 80% of those cases have been linked to international travel

   (D) has been linked to domestic travels

   (E) unknown

32. What does CDC recommend to prevent measles outbreaks?

   (A) cancel international cargoes

   (B) restrict domestic flights

   (C) 95% of a community should be vaccinated

   (D) no international travels

   (E) 50% must stay at home

33. What does "ticking up" mean?

   (A) gradually reducing

   (B) increasing in number

   (C) slowly getting smaller in size

   (D) running out of time

   (E) late

34. Which word is synonymous with "urge"?

(A) implore   (B) discourage   (C) dissuade   (D) veer   (E) deny

Passage 7

It was a fisherman's <u>dwelling</u>, built in a little cove on the sea-shore, and close to the small fishing village of Hardrick, on the coast of Cornwall.

Jacob Williams, its owner, had been a sailor during the early part of his life, but when he was married, he gave up his seafaring life and settled down at Hardrick as a fisherman; and on account of his steady, persevering habits and his former experience, he was looked up to as quite an authority in those parts.

He had three children now, and there was one who was never mentioned, but who was always in his thoughts, who slept in the little churchyard within the sound of the breakers on the shore where he had met his death. Jacob had never been the same man since his sailor-boy had been drowned. There was his little lame daughter Gracie, whose sweet face and gentle ways were a <u>perpetual</u> delight to him, and whose infirmity made her only more dear to his loving, fatherly heart.

from Fisherman's children *by F. M. S.*

35. What is the story about?

(A) about the fishing village on the coast of Cornwall

(B) about the fishermen at Hardrick

(C) about the little cove on the seashore

(D) about the fisherman and his family

(E) about Jacob William's former occupation

36. What does "dwelling" mean as used in the story?

(A) pondering   (B) linger   (C) workplace   (D) school   (E) home

37. The phrase "there was one who was never mentioned, but who was always in his thoughts" implies that the child is _____.

(A) dead

(B) sent to boarding school

(C) adopted by a relative

(D) sent to college

(E) has eloped

38. Based on the story's description, we may assume that Jacob Williams is _____

(A) a beginner and needs more practice

(B) not knowledgeable of the fishing life

(C) arrogant because of his experience as a sailor

(D) well-known and a respectable fisherman

(E) hopeless in his livelihood

39. What is the meaning of the word "perpetual"?

(A) confined within limits

(B) lasting an indefinitely long time

(C) restricted or circumscribed

(D) subject to limitations or conditions

(E) capable of being completely counted

40. Which is synonymous to the word "perpetual"?

(A) bounded   (B) eternal   (C) ceasing   (D) finite   (E) limited

SECTION 4

VERBAL REASONING

Time—30 minutes
60 Questions

Directions: This section is divided into two parts that contain different types of questions. As soon as you have completed part one, answer the questions in part two. You may write in your test booklet. For each answer you select, fill in the corresponding circle on your answer document.

PART ONE

Directions: Each question in part one is made up of a word in capital letters followed by five choices. Choose a word that is most nearly the same in meaning as the word in capital letters.

Example	Answer
SWIFT: (A) clean (B) fancy (C) fast (D) quiet (E) noisy	Ⓐ Ⓑ ● Ⓓ Ⓔ

1. FUNDAMENTAL

   (A) accessory   (B) extrinsic   (C) significant   (D) inessential   (E) minor

2. FURIOUS

   (A) calm   (B) cheerful   (C) gentle   (D) peaceful   (E) enraged

3. FURTIVE

   (A) sneaky   (B) honest   (C) honest   (D) open   (E) truthful

4. GAP

   (A) accord   (B) closure   (C) agreement   (D) crack   (E) juncture

5. GENIAL

   (A) depressed   (B) cheerful   (C) disagreeable   (D) gloomy   (E) mean

6. GENEROUS

   (A) biased   (B) charitable   (C) greedy   (D) inconsiderate   (E) malevolent

7. GENUINE

(A) legitimate (B) doubtful (C) dubious (D) indefinite (E) questionable

8. GERMANE

(A) inappropriate (B) relevant (C) irrelevant (D) unsuitable (E) unrelated

9. GLEAN

(A) dispense (B) gather (C) divide (D) separate (E) spread

10. GLINT

(A) dullness (B) darkness (C) boredom (D) twinkle (E) monotony

11. GLUTTON

(A) shy (B) lazy (C) bashful (D) hog (E) gentle

12. GRACEFUL

(A) characterized by elegance (B) lacking ease in movement

(C) without culture, learning, or refinement (D) with ill manners

(E) showing lack of good social breeding

13. GRATIFY

(A) to disregard on purpose (B) to keep away from

(C) to satisfy one's desires or appetites (D) to keep clear of

(E) to make void or of no effect

14. GRIEVANCE

(A) a high degree of pleasure or enjoyment (B) a power of pleasing or attracting

(C) a complaint against an unjust act (D) the state of being contented

(E) ease of mind

15. GULLIBLE

(A) showing good or outstanding judgment

(B) possessing or exhibiting insight

(C) having or showing keenness of intuition

(D) characterized by or displaying no or little hesitation

(E) easily deceived

16. HAPHAZARD

(A) cautious in one's actions   (B) vigilant or alert or closely observant

(C) thoughtful of others or considerate   (D) without plan or organization

(E) taking heed or mindful

17. HARDSHIP

(A) a personal burden   (B) any means specifically favorable to success

(C) a position of superiority   (D) help or support   (E) means of remedying

18. HASTE

(A) moving or proceeding with less than usual speed

(B) taking or requiring a comparatively long time

(C) to act with speed or hurry

(D) sluggish in nature

(E) dull of perception or understanding

19. HAUGHTY

(A) having a feeling of insignificance   (B) low in rank or importance

(C) scornfully arrogant   (D) courteously respectful   (E) low in height or level

20. HAZARD

(A) freedom from the occurrence or risk of injury

(B) the quality of averting or not causing injury

(C) the action of keeping safe

(D) a positive declaration intended to give confidence

(E) an unavoidable danger or risk

21. HESITATE

(A) to continue steadfastly   (B) to be reluctant   (C) to last or endure tenaciously

(D) to be insistent in a statement   (E) to move or bring forward

22. HIDEOUS

(A) giving great pleasure   (B) socially acceptable or adept   (C) frightful to the senses

(D) delighting the senses or mind   (E) excellent of its kind

23. HINDER

(A) to cause delay   (B) to bring forward in time   (C) to speed up the progress of

(D) to help or encourage to exist or flourish   (E) to advance in rank

24. HOARD

(A) to give out in shares   (B) to pass out or deliver   (C) to accumulate for preservation or future

(D) to divide into distinct phases   (E) to present voluntarily

25. HOMELY

(A) grand in an imposing or impressive way   (B) going beyond what is deserved

(C) commonly seen or known   (D) exceeding the bounds of reason

(E) more complicated or elaborate than necessary

26. IDIOSYNCRASY

(A) normality   (B) peculiarity   (C) usualness   (D) commonality   (E) normalcy

27. IGNOBLE

(A) dignified   (B) grand   (C) lowly   (D) high   (E) reputable

28. ILLUMINATE

(A) enlighten   (B) darken   (C) dull   (D) extinguish   (E) complicate

29. ILLUSTRATE

(A) complicate   (B) confuse   (C) explain   (D) conceal   (E) cover

30. IMBUE

(A) drain   (B) ditch   (C) instill   (D) diminish   (E) empty

PART TWO

Directions: Each question below is made up of a sentence with one or two blanks. One blank indicates that one word is missing. Two blanks indicate that two words are missing. Each sentence is followed by four choices. Select a word or pair of words that will best complete the meaning of the sentence as a whole.

Example   Answer

Ann carried the box carefully so that she would not _____ the pretty glasses.   ●ⒷⒸⒹ

(A) break
(B) fix
(C) open
(D) stop

Example   Answer

When our boat first crashed into the rocks we were _____, but we soon felt   ●ⒷⒸⒹ
_____ when we realized that nobody was hurt.

(A) afraid; relieved
(B) happy; confused
(C) sleepy; sad
(D) sorry; angry

---

31. All the ladies at court waited to see his ____ face, but Catherine was never interested in his looks.

    (A) flawed   (B) dull   (C) immaculate   (D) horrible

32. The debate between two nations is unable to proceed and has reached an ____.

    (A) impasse   (B) resolution   (C) agreement   (D) passage

33. Being childhood friends, it was easy for Claire to notice what Brian's change in behavior ____.

    (A) describes   (B) implies   (C) realizes   (D) demands

34. After receiving her first paycheck, she went to an ____ shopping spree which she will regret later.

    (A) calm   (B) impulsive   (C) deliberate   (D) calculated

35. As there were only ____ ideas, the class representative immediately adjourned the meeting and gave them time to think at home for tomorrow's follow-up meeting.

    (A) bright   (B) intelligent   (C) smart   (D) inane

36. Her actions were misjudged to _____ rage and encourage students to rebel against the faculty.

    (A) block   (B) discourage   (C) incite   (D) dissuade

37. Bethany will be spending her vacation in Asia and travel _____, then surprise everyone with trinkets when she returns.

    (A) incognito   (B) openly   (C) desperately   (D) unmotivated

38. His ____ attitude was not new to the class, so they were surprised when he volunteered for the role.

    (A) indifferent   (B) caring   (C) compassionate   (D) friendly

39. The faculty's decision to shorten the school festival to a two-day event left the student body ____.

    (A) cheerful   (B) indignant   (C) gleeful   (D) pleased

40. The rival company deployed an employee to __ the organization by posing as an intern and sabotaging their projects.

    (A) develop   (B) improve   (C) infiltrate   (D) advance

41. The forest near the shrine is known to be _____ by venomous snakes which is why access is restricted.

    (A) departed   (B) vacated   (C) left   (D) inhabited

42. Billy had an ____ talent for music which is why his parents worked hard to send him to music lessons.

    (A) innate   (B) extrinsic   (C) incidental   (D) lack of

43. Shiela brought the seemingly ____ material thinking it will not affect the finished product.

    (A) dangerous   (B) destructive   (C) innocuous   (D) harmful

44. The goal of the science fair is to encourage young minds to ____ and bring their ideas into reality.

    (A) destroy   (B) damage   (C) innovate   (D) conclude

45. At today's class, everyone was in awe with Kevin, the silent boy, when he shared his ____ into the country's education system.

    (A) ignorance   (B) insight   (C) stupidity   (D) foolishness

46. The tenured employees __ that the newer employees should get more workload so they can ____ off at work.

    (A) insinuated: slack   (B) insinuated: smart   (C) declined: rest   (D) offered: welcome

47. The way he dressed made him look ____ but once you get to know him, you'll ____ his great character.

   (A) original: demand   (B) tasty: damage   (C) pleasing: cancel   (D) insipid: appreciate

48. Christine turned her face and gave an ____ reply saying she'd be ____ off living alone.

   (A) insolent: better   (B) accurate: best   (C) humble: worse   (D) modest: never

49. An ____ will happen after school to ____ class activities for the much-awaited school festival.

   (A) interrogation: dissuade   (B) cooperation: cancel   (C) assembly: integrate   (D) rally: propose

50. The mansion was built in the late 1940s and was __ with __ details from the ceiling to the floors.

   (A) damaged: insipid   (B) adorned: intricate   (C) decorated: intelligent   (D) demolished: complex

51. The faculty was ____ with requests from students to ____ the exams due to the upcoming storm.

   (A) emptied: cancel   (B) inundated: reschedule   (C) started: propose   (D) filled: continue

52. It is that time that she ____ God's mercy to ____ her from embarrassment.

   (A) wrote: pull   (B) declined: push   (C) invoked: rescue   (D) asked: continue

53. An ____ passenger who couldn't get a special item from the menu was ____ by the air marshals which made Rose's flight memorable.

   (A) irate: restrained   (B) calm: deported   (C) rowdy: celebrated   (D) humble: chained

54. Seeing the ____ scene gave him a ____ appetite so he had to skip breakfast.

   (A) motivational: gluttonous   (B) inspiring: great   (C) gross: jaded   (D) dirty: full

55. The rival team ____ every time the home team scores, but it didn't make them ____ their focus.

   (A) scoffed: loose   (B) shouted: lost   (C) jeered: lose   (D) whispered: gain

56. Jubilant is to elated as despondent is to ____.

   (A) exuberant   (B) exultant   (C) joyous   (D) dejected

57. Keen is to sharp as ludicrous is to ____.

   (A) foolish   (B) balanced   (C) calm   (D) secure

58. Laudatory is to praiseful as castigating is to ____.

   (A) insulting   (B) appreciative   (C) commemorative   (D) commendatory

59. Lavish is to economical as sparse is to ____.

   (A) inadequate   (B) abundant   (C) meager   (D) sturdy

60. Lament is to celebrate as applaud is to ____.

   (A) approve   (B) cheer   (C) blame   (D) encourage

SECTION 5

QUANTITATIVE MATH

Time—30 minutes

25 Questions

Directions: Each question is followed by five suggested answers. Read each question and then decide which one of the five suggested answers is best.

Find the row of spaces on your answer document that has the same number as the question. In this row, mark the space having the same letter as the answer you have chosen. You may write in your test booklet.

Example

5,413 – 4,827 =

(A) 586
(B) 596
(C) 696
(D) 1,586
(E) 1,686

The correct answer to this question is lettered A, so space A is marked.

Answer

● Ⓑ Ⓒ Ⓓ Ⓔ

---

1. How many factors does 24 have?

(A) 8   (B) 6   (C) 4   (D) 10   (E) 2

2. If $33 \times a = 297$, then what is $33 - a$?

(A) 35   (B) 27   (C) 33   (D) 24   (E) 30

3. When $z + y = 17$ and $3x + 11z = 40$, what is the value of x?

(A) 102   (B) 120   (C) 201   (D) 140   (E) cannot be determined

4. Based on the table below, approximately how much snow was accumulated during the 7 hours?

Hour	Inches of Snow
1	3.2
2	2.9
3	6.7
4	2.1
5	1.9
6	0.8
7	4.1

(A) 27.1 (B) 21.7 (C) 25.6 (D) 24.3 (E) 22.9

5. Evaluate: 0.0017×46

(A) 0.0782 (B) 0.782 (C) 7.82 (D) 78.2 (E) 782

6. Simplify: $\left(-\dfrac{5}{3}\right)^3$

(A) $\dfrac{5}{3}$ (B) $-\dfrac{5}{3}$ (C) $-\dfrac{125}{9}$ (D) $\dfrac{10}{6}$ (E) $-\dfrac{25}{6}$

7. Which, if there's any, of the following is always true?

(A) the square of any number is greater than that number

(B) if the numerator and denominator of a fraction are increased or decreased by the same amount, then the value of the fraction is unchanged

(C) if the numerator and denominator of a fraction are squared, then the value of the fraction is unchanged

(D) if an odd number is added to an odd number, then the sum is odd

(E) none of the above

8. Evaluate: $(-5) + (-12) + 9 + 14 + 10 \div 2 + 75 - 54 \times 0$

(A) 45 (B) 0 (C) 21 (D) 63 (E) 17

9. If $P < 0$, which of the following is the greatest?

(A) $P - 0$ (B) $P + 1$ (C) $3P + 1$ (D) $5P \times 0$ (E) $\dfrac{P}{P} + 1$

10. Simplify: $\dfrac{3^2 a^2 b^3}{9ab^2}$

(A) ab^3 (B) $3ab^2$ (C) $9a^2b$ (D) ab (E) a^2b

11. Give the next number in the following sequence: 3, 5, 10, 12, 24, 26, 52, 54, __

(A) 108 (B) 98 (C) 86 (D) 76 (E) 102

For questions 12 and 13, please refer to the chart below.

Lila conducted a study to determine what movie genre her coworkers would love to watch for their engagement activity. She was able to get 170 respondents and below is the result.

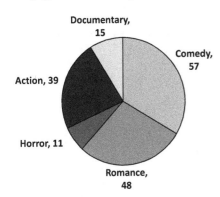

12. What percentage of her coworkers chose Comedy?

(A) 41 (B) 25% (C) 34% (D) 29% (E) 17%

13. What percentage chose Horror and Documentary?

(A) 20% (B) 15% (C) 10% (D) 18% (E) 12%

14. If the sum of the smallest and largest of three consecutive even numbers is 28, what is the value of the second largest number?

(A) 16 (B) 14 (C) 18 (D) 12 (E) 10

15. Evaluate: 9151.324 ÷ 11.2

(A) 817.250 (B) 817.205 (C) 817.025 (D) 817.052 (E) 817.022

16. A line can be represented by $x + 2y = 8$. What is the slope of the line that is perpendicular to it?

(A) 3 (B) $\dfrac{1}{2}$ (C) $-\dfrac{1}{2}$ (D) 2 (E) –2

17. Multiply: $(2i - 3)(3i - 5)$

(A) $6i^2 - 19i + 15$ (B) $6i^2 - 9i + 15$ (C) $6i^2 + i + 15$ (D) $6i^2 + 9i + 15$ (E) $6i^2 - 19i - 15$

18. If the vertex angle of an isosceles triangle is 48°, what is the value of one of its base angles?

(A) 50° (B) 66° (C) 90° (D) 72° (E) 54°

19. One angle of a right triangle has measure 55°. Give the measures of the other two angles.

    (A) 45° and 80°   (B) 30° and 95°   (C) 45° and 45°   (D) 35° and 90°   (E) none of the above

20. A spherical balloon has a diameter of 2 m. Give the volume of the balloon.

    (A) 4.19 m³   (B) 4.91 m³   (C) 4.19 m²   (D) 4.16 m³   (E) 4.11 m²

21. A rectangle has a perimeter of 80 in. The width of the rectangle is 2 in shorter than its length. Give the length of the rectangle.

    (A) 11 in   (B) 24 in   (C) 8 in   (D) 15 in   (E) 21 in

22. The perimeter of a square is 36 cm. What is the area of the square?

    (A) 72 sq in   (B) 9 sq in   (C) 81 sq in   (D) 60 sq in   (E) 56 sq in

23. A line segment has the endpoints (−1, 3) and (4, −2). What is the length of this line segment?

    (A) $2\sqrt{2}$ (B) $6\sqrt{2}$ (C) $5\sqrt{3}$ (D) $2\sqrt{3}$ (E) $5\sqrt{2}$

24. What is the perimeter of a regular hexagon if one side measures 370.8 cm?

    (A) 2228.4 cm   (B) 2242.8 cm   (C) 2222.8 cm   (D) 2224.8 cm   (E) 2284.2 cm

25. At what region in a coordinate plane (5, −11) is placed?

    (A) quadrant I   (B) quadrant II   (C) quadrant III   (D) quadrant IV   (E) x-axis

Answer Key

Section 1

Topic: The value of education to one's success.

Why does one go to school? Why do our parents make efforts to send us to prestigious universities? Is it to be knowledgeable? Is it to be equipped with knowledge and skills we need for the real world? Is it to land a better paying job or is it because there's no other way around it?

Education, undoubtedly, is a treasure nobody can steal from you. From a young age, we were taught that going to school and doing good at school will yield a better future. Does the kind of education or place where you go to matter to one's success?

Many believed that going to the Ivy League schools is your ticket to a successful adult life. Students thrive to meet the qualifications to be able to get in the circle but, does it really define success? Will it mean that those student who are unable to attend these schools will never face success? Your education is one of the tools you may use toward a successful life but there is more to it. As they say, knowledge without wisdom and action is futile. One cannot be successful only because they are smart. Intelligence is a raw material that needs both wisdom and action to mold into something advantageous. Sure, the quality of education may differ depending on the institution but all of them offer knowledge. However, it is your life experiences that will mold your wisdom and character which are not confined in the four walls of a classroom. These things cannot be taught through a lecture but are earned from real life encounters.

A number of successful individuals have proven that finishing graduate school or getting a degree the only tool to success. Therefore, education is important but not the only way. Where you graduated and what degree you hold do not define your path to success. It is you who will pave the way to your own success.

Is going to school still a priority? Yes, knowledge is a prerequisite for someone to exercise wisdom and act. You cannot understand a topic without knowing it which will make it impossible to put something into action.

Gain as much knowledge as you can. As you gain more knowledge, more opportunities will open which will lead to better possibilities in career and personal growth. The price of your education and where you get it do not matter. Later on, with wisdom and experience, you have the freedom to decide which are beneficial to your success.

Section 2

1. C	6. E	11. D	16. A	21. D
2. A	7. A	12. D	17. E	22. C
3. E	8. B	13. C	18. B	23. A
4. C	9. E	14. B	19. A	24. E
5. D	10. A	15. C	20. B	25. B

1. **Answer: C**

    Divide the number of guests by the number of chocolates to know how many packages needed: $55 \div 7 = 7.9$, round it off to 8. Leo needs to buy 8 packages of chocolate, hence the answer is C.

2. **Answer: A**

    Let's convert first the weight of the backpack from kg to lb.: $4.5 \times 2.2 = 9.9$ lb. Next, subtract the weight of the backpack to the weight needed to engage the sensor: $104 - 9.9 = 94.1$ lb. The person sitting on the passenger seat should at least be 94.1 lb, hence the answer is A.

3. **Answer: E**

    Divide: $4053 \div 82 = 49.427$. The answer is E.

4. **Answer: C**

    Let x be the least number and $x + 3$ be the greatest number: $x + 3 = \frac{1}{3}x + 31 \implies x - \frac{1}{3}x = 28 \implies \frac{2}{3}x = 28$ $\implies x = 42$. Substitute the value of x to get the greatest number: $x + 3 = 42 + 3 = 45$. The greatest number is 45, hence the answer is C.

5. **Answer: D**

    To get the perimeter of a regular hexagon is $P = 6s$. We can use this to get the measure of each side: $102 = 6s \implies s = 17$. Let's subtract the length of each side with 2 to get the perimeter of the new figure: $17 - 2 = 15$. $P = 6(15) = 90$. The new perimeter is 90 units, hence the answer is D.

6. **Answer: E**

    It was not indicated what direction their houses are located, nor the direction of Luis's house to Kim's house. There's not enough data to find the distance, hence the answer is E.

7. **Answer: A**

    Let x be the number: $\frac{30}{100}x = 222 \implies x = 740$. Now that we have the number, let's get 80% of 740: $740 \times \frac{80}{100} = 592$. The answer is A.

8. **Answer: B**

    As the value of the denominator in a fraction increases, the quantity it represented decreases, hence the answer is B.

9. **Answer: E**

    To find how long the train take to get to Regalia, use the formula $Time = \frac{Distance}{Speed} = \frac{300}{50} = 6$. The train will travel for 6 hours. If we add 6 hours from the departure time, it is expected to arrive at 3:40 p.m. It will be 10 minutes late, hence the answer is E.

10. Answer: **A**

Let's add all the expenses incurred: \$38,500 + \$1,625 + \$1,975 + \$1,400 = \$43,500. Let's get the 15% of the total expenses: $43{,}500 \times \dfrac{15}{100} = 6{,}525$. Add the result to the expenses: 43,500 + 6,525 = 50,025. She at least must sell the house and lot for \$50,025, hence the answer is A.

11. Answer: **D**

Substitute: $\sqrt{2(7+1)-4(1+2)} = \sqrt{2(8)-4(3)} = \sqrt{16-12} = \sqrt{4} = 2$. The answer is D.

12. Answer: **D**

There's a total of 25 persons in the cheerleading team. There are 15 girls out of 25, so that will be $\dfrac{15}{25}$ or 60%, hence the answer is D.

13. Answer: **C**

Let's find how much Del took out from his bank account: $560 \times \dfrac{20}{100} = 112$. Del had withdrawn \$112. Let's then subtract it from the amount he initially had: 560 – 112 = 448. Del is now left with \$448, hence the answer is C.

14. Answer: **B**

Let x be the percentage. Set up a proportion, then cross multiply: $\dfrac{42}{120} = \dfrac{x}{100} \Rightarrow 120x = 4200 \Rightarrow x = 35$. 42 is 35% of 120, hence the answer is B.

15. Answer: **C**

The numerical expression for the given is 8003.007, hence the answer is C.

16. Answer: **A**

Let's multiply the weight of each golf ball to the total number of golf balls: 0.05 × 12 = 0.6. Let's then subtract the result from the total weight: 0.84 – 0.6 = 0.24. The bag weighs 0.24 kg, hence the answer is A.

17. Answer: **E**

Add all items purchased: 5 + 3 + 9 + 2 + 1 = 20. There was a total of 20 items. There are 9 onions out of 20 items or 9:20, hence the answer is E.

18. Answer: **B**

Subtract the total number of games played with the number of wins to get the number of games where they lost: 27 – 18 = 9. The ratio of wins to losses is 18 to 9. This will 18:9 or 2:1, hence the answer is B.

19. Answer: **A**

Let's get the possible value of k: $k + 3 > 19 \Rightarrow k > 19 - 3 \Rightarrow k > 16$. K is any integer greater than 16, hence the answer is A.

20. **Answer: B**

   Let x be the height of the tree. Set up a proportion, then cross multiply: $\frac{6}{12} = \frac{x}{50} \Rightarrow 12x = 300 \Rightarrow x = 25$. The tree is 25 ft tall, hence the answer is B.

21. **Answer: D**

   Let x be the number of people that attended the fourth game. Let's get the total people that attended the four games. Multiply 4 on the average: 29,500 × 4 = 118,000. There are a total of 118,000 attendees: 22,600 + 27,500 + 35,100 + x = 118,000 ⟹ 85,200 + x = 118,000 ⟹ x = 32,800. There were 32,800 people who attended the fourth game, hence the answer is D.

22. **Answer: C**

   Any point on the surface rotates once each day to a point in space. Each revolution is an angle of 360°. In three days, three revolutions will take place: 360° × 3 = 1080°. The answer is C.

23. **Answer: A**

   To get the area of a rectangle, use the formula $A = l \times w = 15 \times 9 = 135$. The area is 135 m², hence the answer is A.

24. **Answer: E**

   Each corner of a square measure 90° and if a diagonal is drawn across it. It will create two right triangles. Apply the Pythagorean theorem to get the length of the diagonal or the hypotenuse.

   $c = \sqrt{a^2 + b^2} = \sqrt{7^2 + 7^2} = \sqrt{49 + 49} = \sqrt{98} = 7\sqrt{2}$. The diagonal measure $7\sqrt{2}$ in, hence the answer is E.

25. **Answer: B**

   Let's get the total length of pipe needed: 22 × 8 = 176. Divide the result by the length of pipe being sold: 176 ÷ 70 = 3. The plumber needs to buy approximately 3 sections, hence the answer is B.

Section 3

1. D	6. B	11. D	16. C	21. D	26. B	31. C	36. E
2. A	7. C	12. A	17. A	22. A	27. C	32. C	37. A
3. C	8. A	13. C	18. B	23. C	28. A	33. B	38. D
4. C	9. C	14. C	19. B	24. C	29. C	34. A	39. B
5. E	10. C	15. E	20. D	25. B	30. C	35. D	40. B

1. The correct answer is D. The passage described the boys as not well-dressed and are dressed as laborers with ill-fitting and stained clothes. This implied that the young boys do hard labor and are poverty-stricken to be working a laborious job at a young age.

2. The correct answer is A. Ben is described as having a more refined look compared to the other boys, setting aside his current attire. If dressed well, he might be mistaken to be from a well-off family.

3. The correct answer is C. Aristocratic means characteristic of an aristocrat; having the manners, values, or qualities associated with the aristocracy.

4. The correct answer is C. To deface means to mar the surface or appearance of; disfigure.

5. The correct answer is E. It was stated in the passage that the first boy was a boot-black, which means a person employed to polish boots and shoes. Ben's occupation was not stated in the passage, but based on the description of his appearance, he is also a laborer like the first boy.

6. The correct answer is B. Frayed means worn to loose, raveled threads or fibers at the outer surface, edge, or end.

7. The correct answer is C. The passage described the boys as not well-dressed and are dressed as laborers with ill-fitting and stained clothes. This implied that the young boys do hard labor and are poverty-stricken to be working a laborious job at a young age. The most appropriate reaction is to feel pity for them not having the opportunity to enjoy lives being children and complete their education.

8. The correct answer is A. The passage is about the incident of a train carrying hazardous materials that derailed into Montana River which prompted concerns of contamination.

9. The correct answer is C. The incident prompted concerns about contamination. As officials stated, two cars known to be carrying sodium hydro sulfate, which can burn, irritate and cause shortness of breath.

10. The correct answer is C. Officials will continue to monitor the derailment site, and Billings said in a statement that it would shut down city water system intakes fed by the Yellowstone River for the time any pollutant would need to pass and end up downstream.

11. The correct answer is D. Compromised means impaired or diminished in function : weakened, damaged, or flawed.

12. The correct answer is A. To allay means to lessen or relieve; mitigate; alleviate.

13. The correct answer is C. Hazardous means full of risk; perilous; risky.

14. The correct answer is C. Nettie was cheering on her mother and assuring her that there is rest for her. She is full of hope and optimism.

15. The correct answer is E. The mother was complaining of her hardships and that no one can endure forever. She talked about how she feels giving up. Opposite to Nettie, she feels hopeless and negative.

16. The correct answer is C. Weary means physically or mentally exhausted by hard work, exertion, strain, etc.; fatigued; tired.

17. The correct answer is A. Jaded is an adjective which means worn out or wearied, as by overwork or overuse. In this sentence, the word jaded describes the noun "hearts".

18. The correct answer is B. The entire passage presented how Nettie has full of faith that God will provide rest.

19. The correct answer is B. Faint lacking brightness, vividness, clearness, loudness, strength, etc.

20. The correct answer is D. Considering their family traveled from France to India and employed the services of a nurse and a servant to watch over their luggage, we can assume that Mr. and Mrs. Halley are well-off.

21. The correct answer is D. This behavior is mostly seen from someone who is frightened, which the passage stated that young Charles was frightened at the noise and took refuge in the embrace of his mother.

22. The correct answer is A. Considerable size means rather large or great in size, distance, extent, etc.

23. The correct answer is C. Sultry means oppressively hot and close or moist; sweltering.

24. The correct answer is C. Maurice, the first child mentioned and the eldest among the three, is 10 years old as mentioned in the passage.

25. The correct answer is B. The passage was about a story of a firefighter and his wife's answered prayer to have a child after a long period of waiting.

26. The correct answer is B. The story is touching and heartwarming that a child has been taken in by a couple who had been waiting for her will love her like their own.

27. The correct answer is C. The Safe Haven Baby Box is a device that allows someone to safely and anonymously surrender a child—no questions asked.

28. The correct answer is A. Anonymously means without giving a name.

29. The correct answer is C. "Beyond words" is a phrase that expresses an extreme emotional response, such as joy, thankfulness, shock, or even anger. To be loved beyond words means to receive overwhelming love.

30. The correct answer is C. The passage gives us helpful information on the current measles outbreak and recommends that 95% of the community must be vaccinated to prevent such outbreaks.

31. The correct answer is C. Eighty-eight percent of those cases have been linked to international travel. Most patients had not been vaccinated.

32. The correct answer is C. To best prevent measles outbreaks, 95% of a community should be vaccinated, according to the CDC.

33. The correct answer is B. Ticking up means to increase, or to increase something.

34. The correct answer is A. To urge means to press, push, or hasten (the course, activities, etc.).

35. The correct answer is D. The story talks about Jacob Williams, a former sailor, who settled as a fisherman when he married and had his lovely family.

36. The correct answer is E. Dwelling is used as a noun in the story which referred to a place of residence; abode; home.

37. The correct answer is A. The phrase meant that the child has died, but Jacob Williams always commemorates his memory.

38. The correct answer is D. The story stated that on account of his steady, persevering habits and his former experience, he was looked up to as quite an authority in those parts which meant he is renowned and successful.

39. The correct answer is B. Perpetual means continuing or enduring forever; everlasting.

40. The correct answer is B. Perpetual means continuing or enduring forever; everlasting. Other synonyms are eternal and infinite.

Section 4

1. C	11. D	21. B	31. C	41. D	51. B
2. E	12. A	22. C	32. A	42. A	52. C
3. A	13. C	23. A	33. B	43. C	53. A
4. D	14. C	24. C	34. B	44. C	54. C
5. B	15. E	25. C	35. D	45. B	55. C
6. B	16. D	26. B	36. C	46. A	56. D
7. A	17. A	27. C	37. A	47. D	57. A
8. B	18. C	28. A	38. A	48. A	58. A
9. B	19. C	29. C	39. B	49. C	59. B
10. D	20. E	30. C	40. C	50. B	60. C

1. The correct answer is C. Fundamental means serving as, or being an essential part of, a foundation or basis; basic; underlying.

2. The correct answer is E. Furious means full of fury, violent passion, or rage; extremely angry; enraged.

3. The correct answer is A. Furtive means taken, done, used, etc., surreptitiously or by stealth; secret.

4. The correct answer is D. Gap means a break or opening, as in a fence, wall, or military line; breach.

5. The correct answer is B. Genial means warmly and pleasantly cheerful; cordial.

6. The correct answer is B. Generous means liberal in giving or sharing; unselfish.

7. The correct answer is A. Genuine means possessing the claimed or attributed character, quality, or origin; not counterfeit; authentic; real.

8. The correct answer is B. Germane means closely or significantly related; relevant; pertinent.

9. The correct answer is B. Glean means to gather slowly and laboriously, bit by bit.

10. The correct answer is D. Glint means a tiny, quick flash of light.

11. The correct answer is D. Glutton means a person who eats and drinks excessively or voraciously.

12. The correct answer is A. Graceful means characterized by elegance or beauty of form, manner, movement, or speech; elegant.

13. The correct answer is C. To gratify means to give pleasure to (a person or persons) by satisfying desires or humoring inclinations or feelings.

14. The correct answer is C. Grievance means a complaint, as against an unjust or unfair act.

15. The correct answer is E. Gullible means easily deceived or cheated.

16. The correct answer is D. Haphazard means characterized by lack of order or planning, by irregularity, or by randomness; determined by or dependent on chance; aimless.

17. The correct answer is A. Hardship means an instance or cause of this; something hard to bear, as a deprivation, lack of comfort, or constant toil or danger.

18. The correct answer is C. To hasten means to move or act with haste; proceed with haste; hurry.

19. The correct answer is C. Haughty means disdainfully proud; scornfully arrogant; snobbish; supercilious.

20. The correct answer is E. Hazard means an unavoidable danger or risk, even though often foreseeable.

21. The correct answer is B. To hesitate means to be reluctant or wait to act because of fear, indecision, or disinclination.

22. The correct answer is C. Hideous means horrible or frightful to the senses; repulsive; very ugly.

23. The correct answer is A. To hinder means to cause delay, interruption, or difficulty in; hamper; impede.

24. The correct answer is C. To hoard means to accumulate money, food, or the like, in a hidden or carefully guarded place for preservation, future use.

25. The correct answer is C. Homely means lacking in physical attractiveness; not beautiful; unattractive. It means commonly seen or known.

26. The correct answer is B. Idiosyncrasy means a characteristic, habit, mannerism, or the like, that is peculiar to an individual.

27. The correct answer is C. Ignoble means of low character, aims, etc.; mean; base.

28. The correct answer is A. To illuminate means to supply or brighten with light; light up. It can also mean to enlighten, as with knowledge.

29. The correct answer is C. To illustrate means to furnish (a book, magazine, etc.) with drawings, pictures, or other artwork intended for explanation, elucidation, or adornment. It also means to clarify one's words, writings, etc., with examples:

30. The correct answer is C. To imbue means to impregnate or inspire, as with feelings, opinions, etc.

31. The correct answer is C. Immaculate means free from spot or stain; spotlessly clean. It also means free from moral blemish or impurity; pure; undefiled.

32. The correct answer is A. An impasse is a position or situation from which there is no escape; deadlock.

33. The correct answer is B. To imply means to indicate or suggest without being explicitly stated.

34. The correct answer is B. Impulsive means actuated or swayed by emotional or involuntary impulses.

35. The correct answer is D. Inane means lacking sense, significance, or ideas; silly.

36. The correct answer is C. To incite means to stir, encourage, or urge on; stimulate or prompt to action.

37. The correct answer is A. Incognito means with the real identity concealed.

38. The correct answer is A. Indifferent means without interest or concern; not caring; apathetic.

39. The correct answer is B. Indignant means feeling, characterized by, or expressing strong displeasure at something considered unjust, offensive, insulting, or base.

40. The correct answer is C. To infiltrate means to filter into or through; permeate. It also means to move into (an organization, country, territory, or the like) surreptitiously and gradually, especially with hostile intent.

41. The correct answer is D. To inhabit means to exist or be situated within; dwell in.

42. The correct answer is A. Innate means existing in one from birth; inborn; native.

43. The correct answer is C. Innocuous means not harmful or injurious; harmless.

44. The correct answer is C. To innovate means to introduce something new; make changes in anything established.

45. The correct answer is B. Insight means an instance of apprehending the true nature of a thing, especially through intuitive understanding.

46. The correct answer is A. To insinuate means to suggest or hint slyly. To slack off means to do something more slowly or with less energy than before.

47. The correct answer is D. Insipid means without distinctive, interesting, or stimulating qualities; vapid. It also means without sufficient taste to be pleasing, as food or drink; bland. To appreciate means to value or regard highly; place a high estimate on.

48. The correct answer is A. Insolent means boldly rude or disrespectful; contemptuously impertinent; insulting. Better off means in a more desirable or advantageous position, especially in financial terms.

49. The correct answer is C. An assembly means a group of persons gathered together, usually for a particular purpose, whether religious, political, educational, or social. To integrate means to bring together or incorporate (parts) into a whole.

50. The correct answer is B. Adorned means decorated or beautified, as by ornaments. Intricate means complex; complicated; hard to understand, work, or make.

51. The correct answer is B. To inundate means to overwhelm. To reschedule means to schedule for another or later time.

52. The correct answer is C. To invoke to call for with earnest desire; make supplication or pray for. To rescue means to free or deliver from confinement, danger, or difficulty.

53. The correct answer is A. Irate means angry; enraged. To restrain means to prevent (someone or something) from doing something; keep under control or within limits.

54. The correct answer is C. Gross means indelicate, indecent, obscene, or vulgar. Jaded means worn out or wearied, as by overwork or overuse.

55. The correct answer is C. To jeer means to treat with scoffs or derision; mock. To lose means to fail to keep, preserve, or maintain; not to be confused with loose and loss.

56. The correct answer is D. The first word pair are synonyms. Jubilant means feeling or showing great joy, satisfaction, or triumph; rejoicing; exultant. Synonyms are elated and euphoric. Despondent means feeling or showing profound hopelessness, dejection, discouragement, or gloom. Synonyms are dejected and glum.

57. The correct answer is A. The first word pair are synonyms. Keen is characterized by strength and distinctness of perception; extremely sensitive or responsive. Synonyms are sharp and sensitive. Ludicrous means causing laughter because of absurdity; provoking or deserving derision; ridiculous; laughable. Synonyms are foolish and absurd.

58. The correct answer is A. The first word pair are synonyms. Laudatory means containing or expressing praise. Synonyms are commendatory and praiseful. To castigate means to criticize or reprimand severely. Synonyms are insulting and offensive.

59. The correct answer is B. The first word pair are antonyms. Lavish means using or giving in great amounts; prodigal (often followed by of). Antonyms are economical and reasonable. Sparse means thinly scattered or distributed. Antonyms are abundant and plentiful.

60. The correct answer is C. The first word pair are antonyms. To lament means to feel or express sorrow or regret for. Antonyms are to celebrate and praise. To applaud means to express approval; give praise; acclaim. Antonyms are to blame and censure.

Section 5

1. A	6. C	11. A	16. D	21. E
2. D	7. E	12. C	17. A	22. C
3. E	8. B	13. B	18. B	23. E
4. B	9. E	14. B	19. D	24. D
5. A	10. D	15. C	20. A	25. D

1. Answer: **A**

   The factors of 24 are (1,24), (2,12), (3,8), (4,6). There's a total of 8 factors for 24, hence the answer is A.

2. Answer: **D**

   Let's find the value of a: $33 \times a = 297 \implies a = 9$. Substitute: $33 - 9 = 24$. The answer is D.

3. Answer: **E**

   There's not enough information provided to get the value of x, hence the answer is E.

4. Answer: **B**

   Add the snow accumulated throughout the 7 hours: $3.2 + 2.9 + 6.7 + 2.1 + 1.9 + 0.8 + 4.1 = 21.7$

   The accumulated snow is approximately 21.7 inches, hence the answer is B.

5. Answer: **A**

   Multiply: $0.0017 \times 46 = 0.0782$. The answer is A.

6. Answer: **C**

   Distribute the exponent to the numerator and the denominator, and maintain the negative sign, since when a negative integer is raised to the third power, it will result to a negative integer: $-\dfrac{5^3}{3^3} = -\dfrac{125}{9}$. The answer is C.

7. **Answer: E**

We may plug in an example to verify if any of the statements was true. For option A, it's untrue for the number 1, since 1 raised to the power of 1 is still 1. For option B, let's have $\frac{1}{2}$, if we add 1 to the numerator and to the denominator, it will yield $\frac{2}{3}$, which is a different value from $\frac{1}{2}$. Option C is also false. For option D, if an odd number is added with another odd number, the result will be an even number. There's no true statement, hence the answer is E.

8. **Answer: B**

Any integer multiplied by 0, the result is 0, hence the answer is B.

9. **Answer: E**

Option A to D, either has a negative result or 0. Option E, on the other hand, will yield 2, since any number (aside from 0) divided by that number will be 1 and 1 + 1 = 2. The answer is E.

10. **Answer: D**

According to Quotient rules with same base $a^n \div a^m = a^{n-m}$. $\frac{3^2 a^2 b^3}{9ab^2} = \frac{9a^{2-1}b^{3-2}}{9} = ab$. The answer is D.

11. **Answer: A**

The sequence indicates that you need to add 2 on the first number and then multiply the sum with 2. If we follow this, the next number will be 108, hence the answer is A.

12. **Answer: C**

There are 57 respondents who chose Comedy out of 170: $\frac{57}{170}$ = 0.34 or 34%. The answer is C.

13. **Answer: B**

Add the number of respondents who chose Horror and Documentary: 11 + 15 = 26, that will be 26 out of 170 respondents: $\frac{26}{170}$ = 0.15 or 15%. The answer is B.

14. **Answer: B**

Let x be the smallest number, $x + 2$ the second largest number and $x + 4$ be the largest number: $x + x + 4 = 28 \Rightarrow 2x = 24 \Rightarrow x = 12$. Substitute: $x + 2 = 12 + 2 = 14$. The second largest number is 14, hence the answer is B.

15. **Answer: C**

Divide: 9151.324 ÷ 11.2 = 817.0825. The quotient is 817.025, hence the answer is C.

16. **Answer: D**

Let's solve for y: $x + 2y = 8 \Rightarrow 2y = -x + 8 \Rightarrow y = -\frac{1}{2}x + 4$. The slope of this line is $-\frac{1}{2}$. The slope perpendicular to it is the negative reciprocal, which is 2, hence the answer is D.

17. Answer: A

Multiply: $(2i - 3)(3i - 5) = (2i)(3i) + (2i)(-5) + (-3)(3i) + (-3)(-5) = 6i^2 - 10i - 9i + 15 = 6i^2 - 19i + 15$. The answer is A.

18. Answer: B

In an isosceles triangle, the base angles are the angles that are opposite of the side that have equal measure. All three angles of a triangle add up to 180°. Let's subtract the value of the vertex angle from 180°: $180 - 48 = 132$. Let's divide the difference by two to get the value of each angle of the base: $132 \div 2 = 66$. The value of one of the bases is 66°, hence the answer is B.

19. Answer: D

A right triangle has an angle that measure 90°. All triangles have three angles that add up to 180°. We already have the given angles of 55° and 90°. To get the other angle, add the other two angles and subtract the result from 180°: $55 + 90 = 145$, $180 - 145 = 35$. The other two angles are 35° and 90°, hence the answer is D.

20. Answer: A

To get the volume of the spherical balloon, use the formula $V = \frac{4}{3}\pi r^3$, where r is the radius. The radius is half of a diameter, so the radius is 1. Solve for the volume: $V = \frac{4}{3}\pi(1)^3 = \frac{4}{3}\pi = 4.19$. The volume is 4.19 m³, hence the answer is A.

21. Answer: E

To get the perimeter of a rectangles, we can use the formula $P = 2l + 2w$. We can also use this to get the dimensions: $80 = 2l + 2(l - 2) \Rightarrow 80 = 2l + 2l - 4 \Rightarrow 84 = 4l \Rightarrow l = 21$. The length of the rectangle is 21 in, hence the answer is E.

22. Answer: C

To get the perimeter of a square, we can use the formula $P = 4s$. We can also use this to get the dimensions: $36 = 4s \Rightarrow s = 9$. Now that we have the dimension of the square, solve for the area: $A = s^2 = 9^2 = 81$. The area of the square is 81 square cm, hence the answer is C.

23. Answer: E

To get length of the line segment with two given points, use the formula $D = \sqrt{(x_2 - x_1)^2 + (y_2 - y_1)^2} = \sqrt{(4 - (-1))^2 + (-2 - 3)^2} = \sqrt{(5)^2 + (-5)^2} = \sqrt{25 + 25} = \sqrt{50} = 5\sqrt{2}$. The answer is E.

24. Answer: D

To get the perimeter of a regular hexagon, use the formula $P = 6s = 6(370.8) = 2224.8$. The perimeter is 2,224.8 cm, hence the answer is D.

25. Answer: D

Quadrant IV is defined as a point placed in a coordinate plane that has a positive x-axis and negative y-axis, hence the answer is D.

SSAT Report

Scoring Methodology

On the **Middle and Upper Level SSAT**, a point is awarded for each correct answer, a quarter of a point is subtracted for each incorrect answer, and no points are awarded or deducted for omitted questions.

On the **Elementary Level SSAT**, a point is awarded for each correct answer and there is no penalty for incorrect answers.

Score Report Breakdown

Personal Information

The score report header details the student's basic information—name, address, date of birth, gender, etc. Enrollment Management Association (EMA) will have scored the student at the grade displayed as indicated during registration. Please note that while gender is listed, SSAT scores are not gender-specific.

Total Score Summary

This section lists the two total scores.

"Your score" is the total scaled score, and the pointer indicates where the student's score is between the highest and lowest possible score. We also provide the average score for additional context.

The **total percentile** is on the right, comparing the student's scaled score to other SSAT test takers. This score shows the percentage of students that the student scored equal to or higher. For example, a 67th percentile indicates that the student scored equal to or higher than sixty-seven percent of test-takers in their grade.

Section Scores

In this section, EMA breaks score information into verbal reasoning, quantitative (math), and reading segments. Similar to the total score, a scaled score and percentile are shown, along with the average score. We also provide a score range; students who retest within a short period will likely score within this range. A breakdown explaining the main types of questions follows, including the number of questions answered correctly, incorrectly, and unanswered.

Here's a sample SSAT Report

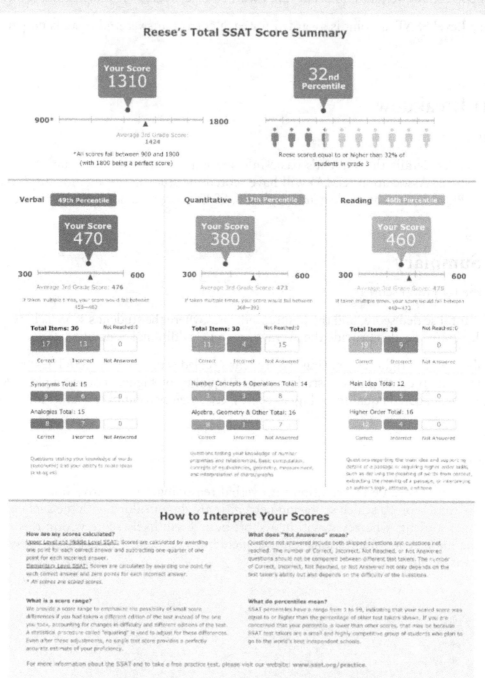

Printed in the USA
CPSIA information can be obtained
at www.ICGtesting.com
JSHW060253230124
55804JS00009B/13